#Jubilee Fever 2020
A Novelty

by

Bob Levis

"Change or Stay Chained"

Levis Productions, ltd.

2019

Dedicated to:

Librarians who care, civil rights attorneys, investigative journalists, whistle-blowers, & labor organizers, especially I.W.W.'s wobblie Bruce Duncan "Utah" Phillips (May 15, 1935 – May 23, 2008).

Solidarity, June 30, 1917.   The Hand That Will Rule the World—One Big Union.

Table of Contents:

Chapter 1 - It's happening, finally!   3

Chapter 2 - The Flotilla   15

Chapter 3 - The Dover Dirge   23

Chapter 4 - "Old Man River"   29

Chapter 5 - Dexter's Vision   35

Chapter 6 - God & Country   43

Chapter 7 - A Most Unhappy Fella   51

Chapter 8 - "It's An Epidemic!"   57

Chapter 9 - Southern Hospitality, AKA Tent City   63

Chapter 10 – "Beyond the Pale"   69

Chapter 11 – Cuffed & Cornered   81

Chapter 12 – Armaggedon Avoided by Consensus   91

Illustrations:

Front Cover Credit: *Butterfly* by Albert Bierstadt (c.1900)
Back Cover Credit: *The Rising Tide* by Felix Vallotton (1913)

Dedication: *The Hand That Will Rule the World-One Big Union/I.W.W. Journal-Solidarity, Jun. 30, 1917* by Ralph Chaplin   iii

Chapter 1: *Skyscrapers* by Charles Sheeler (1922)   2

Chapter 2: *Colonial Policy* by Pavel Filonov (1926)   14

Chapter 3: *Bhopal* (1984)   22

Chapter 4: *Tombs in the Desert* by Nicholas Roerich (1930)   28

Chapter 5: *Fire Dance (Upa upa)* by Paul Gauguin (1891)
Devil (Diabel) by Jan Matejko (c.1890)   34

Chapter 6: *Rush Hour* by Max Weber   42

Chapter 7: *John Brown* by John Steuart Curry (1939)
The Hanged Man... by Felicien Rops (1867)   50

Chapter 8: *Thunder God (Endo)* by Katsushika Hokusai (1847)   56

Chapter 9: *Tents* by Nicholas Roerich (1909)   62

Chapter 10: *Sacrifice of Isaac* by Caravaggio (1598)
A Packed House by Al Jazeera (23 November, 2009)   68

Chapter 11: *Greed (Avarita)* by Pieter Bruegel the Elder (c.1560)   80

Chapter 12: Japanese Ghost-Katsushika Hokusai(c.1850)
Pater-devil-Nicholas Roerich(1912)   90

Acknowledgement

Special thanks to contributing editor and tech guy Tony Bly without whom this effort would not have been nearly as entertaining to work on and, quite simply, would not have been. Tony coined the genre "a novelty". Originally conceived as a "sound-byte", that is, sitting around a fire and telling a story, when we tried to upload to an audible book we were asked to first supply the text. I had only spoken the first chapter from notes so we used the modern tool of voice recognition and transcription. We soon had a text which, of course, required punctuation, etc...but that was easily enough accomplished and "Voila!" we had a novelty!

Foreword

#Jubilee Fever 2020 was initially intended as an Audio Book, or, as the author uses the term, a Sound-Byte.

This Sound-Byte project was no easy matter because an audio recording is not necessarily ready for 'prime-time' even after the last word in the last chapter had been digitilized(not by a long shot). Untold hours of primping, fixing, adjusting and editing the soundtrack was required to hone it towards perfection.

Since neither Bob nor myself had any experience operating a software audio editing program, we had to go through several weeks of mind-boggling learning and working with this wonderful but sometimes baffling computer program.

Upon conclusion of this task, we were struck with a numbing realization: *the audio book could not be produced unless a corresponding paperback existed* which explains the reason why you are holding this book in your hands at this moment.

We sincerely hope that as the proud owner of the printed edition this doesn't stop you from listening to Bob's vocal rendering of *#Jubilee Fever 2020*. It will be well worth your while since he is both an entertaining performer and at the same time, a fine writer.

So, I conclude that, in one way or another, you will enjoy the story.

Tony Bly, July 18, 2019.

Preface

Several months ago my son came off the desert with a cast iron fire pit in the back of his pick-up truck which he'd found abandoned by the side of the road. He placed it in the corner of our front yard. A few nights later, due to unseasonably chilly night weather, we began to have fires with scraps of wood we gathered. Usually began shortly after sunset the routine quickly became ritual. Once the fires began to blaze, neighbors, few of whom I'd known before, either walked or drove by and exchanged greetings. Several stopped and added firewood to a pile by the pit. Before long I recognized that fire is a basic and powerful element. Earth, air, water, and fire! I realized that for too long there had been something lacking in my daily routine. "Elementary, my dear reader!" It got me thinking. One of my very first jobs in show biz was with The Merv Griffin Show whose producer was Bob Shanks. Mr. Shanks wrote a terrific book about the history of television. He called it "The Cool Fire". He was referring to how the blinking bluish light emanating from the tube had replaced the physical fire and now, instead of building camp fires, families sat around a machine that told stories. Upon further reflection(sitting around our fire, of course,) I realized that no matter how important had been Bob's book much of it had quickly become obsolete with the advent of digitalization, computers and the internet. The lesson? Change comes no matter what. Sometimes in a split second, sometimes over centuries. But it does come. We humans do not have control over change. But, we might be able to harness some change if we act diligently. The next thought that followed was another question. Do we have control over chains? The chains that lock us into stupid war after stupid war. Conclusion? Yes, we do have control if only we utilize our grey matter.

Focusing on that thought I began thinking in the tried and true story mode of "What if?". What if soldiers refused to follow orders and instead of invading sovereign nations they just said, "No thanks. Do it yourself."? What if they collectively flatly refused to march? ... if they quit serving the weapons manufacturers who were so obviously bilking the public? What if students refused to pay their outrageous loans and instead declared education free? What if, what if...countless possibilities sparked out from the fires. One night my granddaughter asked me, "How much is a billion?" I had to do some calculating. Wow, a billion is one thousand million! Does one person need that much money to get by? What kind of system have we created where thousands can go hungry and we have billionaires? Why are soldiers so readily defending this inequity? Indeed, what if a jubilee was declared globally. A moratorium on wars, debt, hate...what if? So began the piecing together of #Jubilee Fever 2020.

Bob L. *September* 12th, 2019.

#Jubilee Fever 2020

A Novelty

NSA Headquarters NYC

#Jubilee Fever 2020

Chapter 1
"It's happening, finally!"

Sunday, July 26, 2020

Picture this: a hundred-year old brick building comes to life on a hot, steamy summer morning in Louisville, Kentucky. A soft breeze from the Ohio River a few blocks away floats like a butterfly down Muhammad Ali Boulevard towards the inviting rectangular edifice known by the locals simply as "the gardens". Parked outside are several pickup trucks loaded down with lumber and also a few familiar 1960s VW hippie vans. Though it's just past the crack of dawn, there's an anthill of activity. Young men, young women heft two-by-fours on their shoulders and carry them through the colonnaded front entrance. The distinct sound of hammers pounding nails echo up and down the vast foyer. Inside the cavernous hall buzz saws grind through the timber. A finished kiosk has just been erected and several folks are decorating with green, gold and blue bunting. Meredith Ann Baker, a slight middle-aged woman stands with her fists dug into her hips. She's nodding approval. She's dressed in purple as is her custom. She's the den mother of a group of activists known as Code Purple.

"We need at least 50 of these," she addresses her coworkers. She speaks with a slight New... no, it's a Long Island accent, "Each booth will have its own sandwich board out front, a Jubilee poster on one side and a description of whatever workshop or teach-in on the other... you know, the time, the place, the list of expert panelists..."

A young man with a top hat stovepipe style outfitted in a sandwich board approaches. Meredith smiles at the group and says, "Haven't I always said, 'timing is everything'. Glen, good to see you. Let's take a look at... oh....!" Bright yellow lettering against a maroon background the poster on the sandwich board reads, "Jubilee 2020, August 4th through the 11th, Louisville, Kentucky. Fifty Notions for all Nations, Music, Food, **Brainpower**, $5 admission."

Meredith speaks into a small microphone that hugs her cheek. In her ear is a barely perceptible earbud. "Oh, it looks so cool. Brad must've been up all night. How many? Just 50, that's all? No, no, no, no. Each workshop will need maybe 200, maybe even 300." She motions to the lad in the sandwich board to turn around so she can read the other side of the poster which says, "Workshop/Teach-In, Corporate Grooming. Thursday, August 4th, 4.00 to 6:00 PM and beyond. Panelists, Nomi Prins, Richard Wolf, Michael Hudson, Joseph Stiglitz: topic, **How the Corporate Gatekeepers Filter Out Your Radical Ideas**." Meredith squints, she reads the small, print at the bottom, "Always remember everything is possible. Oh good. End on a positive note. I like that. Oh, this is terrific." She listens than interjects," What? He didn't say that. No, no, no. He was just kidding you." She turns to the group, "You know what the printer said? 'It's all about the Benjamins, baby.' No, no. He's getting a good retainer. He'll keep working. Just tell him to keep the presses rolling. We... we have to get these out. He's a good man. You just be diplomatic."

A camera crew approaches. Lydia Baez calls out to Meredith, "Is this what I think it is?" Lydia speaks with a dollop of a southern drawl. She motions to her cameraman to get a shot of the poster.

"Oh, you got your scoop," says Meredith. "Come on, gal, your viewers will be the very first to get a gander of our posters. They're hot off the presses." Meredith touches one of the posters and pulls her hand away abruptly jokingly blowing on her fingers, "Oh, burnt my little pinky, I did." She pivots, "Just like I told the mayor, we're bringing business to your burg."

Lydia shakes her head, "The mayor wants you here, that's for sure. But the governor would just as soon shut you down. Kit and caboodle."

Meredith sighs, "Oh, no. Are they still fighting? No, no. We're going to bring more business to this town than the Derby. What's... what's wrong with the governor? I mean, we're going to have concerts every night-sold out. Hotels at full capacity. Workshops running almost 24 seven."

"Hey," says Lydia, "I'm going to cover as much as I can. I like this idea of the Jubilee. I really do."

"Okay, I'll tell you what," says Meredith, "the restaurants better have enough food to feed everybody."

"But here's the thing," Lydia counters, "the governor says you are all socialists."

"Oh, more labels!" says Meredith defeated almost, "What's wrong with him? I mean, libertarians, communists, anarchists, we're just people. You know how much one of these four-color posters costs? Multiply that by thousands and you come up with what? Capitalism 101."

"Hey, I hear you," says Lydia.

"... and I'll tell you one thing else," continues Meredith, "I'm telling you that we are here to strengthen this system-not weaken it, but changes need to be made and that's why we're gathering. We can't have the governor's cronies, like the Disney CEO, making a thousand times as much as the working stiff who cleans bubble gum off the sidewalk. We have weapons at our disposal."

Lydia's ears crop, "What weapons? This may be a scoop. What weapons are you talking about?"

"Not military weapons. I'm talking about strategic economic weapons such as strikes. You know, just like school teachers all around the country have gone on strike. These are working class people. They demand equal rights, equal pay. And the boycott. Obviously, we'll be doing boycotts on any corporation that doesn't comply and tries to give their CEOs these huge bonuses. It's not going to happen anymore. These things are destroying our way of life and we're going to change it."

"Okay. I'm all for you. Like I said, I'll cover whatever I can," says Lydia, "but I got to tell you something. I read your 50 notions for all nations, Meredith, some of these are just pie in the sky."

Meredith ruffled, "Okay. I understand that some are pie in the sky, but they're just little simple things that need to be addressed and that's why we're having this conference. We have to start taking care of the problems of this planet. What's the governor doing? Ask him that, or I'll ask him myself. What's he doing about air pollution and water pollution? Just look, you're a few blocks away. The Ohio river is the most polluted river in the country and 3 million people get their drinking water from this river. I can guarantee you, Lydia, in a few years when drinking water becomes scarce, there will be chaos. If he doesn't start to take care of this he's a fool..."

"Well, I grant you that," says Lydia. "I will be covering the workshops and I'll tell you what... we... I look forward to seeing all these world class experts. I want to hear what's going on. I really do."

Just then, Robert McGrath, an internationally recognized naturalist walks by followed by several others. Robert sports an outsized backpack.

Meredith calls out to him, "Bobby, Bobby, stop here a minute. I want to introduce you to Lydia Baez. She's the local anchor news lady I told you about. She'll be covering our convention."

McGrath bristles, "Convention! Meredith, Meredith, not a convention. I told you conventions are for rich white old democrats and rich white old republicans who flail away with their noisemakers and wave flags. We're having a world's fair. Ms. Baez," Bobby tips his baseball cap towards Lydia, "I am here to tell you that we're going to be making some major changes and major announcements in the next couple of days. Take a look at my backpack here. We're just going in to demonstrate it. It's a completely self-sustaining home and just 73 and a half pounds. Come on into the auditorium. I'll show you a demo."

Meredith blocks Lydia just momentarily, "Hey, before you go, can you take some of these card size handouts, the short version of 50 notions for all nations."

Lydia stands back, "Listen, I can't take your literature. I really can't. I'm a journalist. I have to maintain some sort of balance."

"Oh," Meredith apologizes with a gesture. She says, "I'm sorry. At least you called it our literature and not our propaganda. Thanks. Come on by later and I'll tell you about all the different venues for the concerts and who's playing where."

"All right, I'll be back, shouts Lydia as she trails off, "Good luck with the posters."

" *

In downtown New York City there stands a tall, white, windowless structure overlooking Pace University and the Brooklyn Bridge. Thousands of people pass by almost every hour but few stop to ponder what exactly goes on inside this bland but ominous building stretching 25, 30, 35 floors into the sky. A peak inside reveals floor after floor of computers collecting data on each and every American citizen. You own a cell phone, uh? Your data is being collected. Someone inside this building can pinpoint when you call your Aunt Ida-where you are and where she is. Out for a drink at the local pub? Someone inside this building knows that you just ordered a pint of Guinness and put it on your credit card. Surveillance Capitalism 101. Do you own a computer? Forget about any privacy whatsoever. That little contraption can rat you out in a nanosecond. Yes, you. You looked at some porn last month while your wife was visiting her mother. Thought nobody would ever find out? You voluntarily joined Facebook, Instagram, Pinterest. Guess what? That little screen in front of you knows what you are going to order for breakfast. Yeah. Think about it.

On the 24th floor of this mysterious obelisk in downtown Gotham, a young man in his late twenties, Jacob Charles, sits in his cubicle with his feet up on his desk. He's chewing nonchalantly on a plastic straw as is his habit. He watches a screen on his desk. Across a narrow aisle his friend and colleague in arms, Todd Marcher, jokes with someone on his cell phone. Jacob notices something on his screen and tries to get

Todd's attention, "Hey, Todd, take a gander at your screen."

Todd puts down his phone, "What's up, my man?"

"It's happening again," says Jacob. "Check out your coordinates. 41.88 North, 87.63 West. It's another cluster."

Todd looks at his screen while making adjustments, "What time is it there?"

Jacob says, "Just an hour difference. 8:00 AM."

Todd nods knowingly," Well, so it's probably just a rush hour fender-bender."

"Yeah," Jacob scoffs, "On Sunday? Come on."

"Oh, what...," says Todd defensively, "What should we do? Call in the cavalry? You nervous Nellie pussy."

"Hey, mock me all you want, prick face," retorts Jacob, "This is different."

"Yeah. How so?" challenges Marcher.

"It ain't just a fender bender. It's in a park. It's Sunday. Cars probably aren't even allowed," Jacob asserts.

"Really," Todd alerts, "Let's take a little closer look. Let me zoom in."

"There. You see a swarm on the lower right. Activity. It's like a beehive," Jacob points.

"Oh yeah, you're right," says Todd. "We better call in the boss. What d'ya think?"

"Yeah."

Todd Marcher hits a button on his desk. Only moments later General Hikeover, a stocky man in his mid-fifties with a buzz cut walks down the corridor. Todd and Jacob both sit at attention. "Gentlemen, someone just called me-cold blue."

"On the radar screen, Sir," Todd answers, "there's a cluster I noticed that you might want to see."

Jacob's smarts, "I saw it first."

Todd ignores him, "It's like the chatter we showed you last week, 10 days ago, right after the Democratic Convention, but this is more pronounced."

The general squints at the screen, "I thought you told me that was just some flotsam after the DNC."

"Well, yeah, that's what we thought," offers Jacob, "but this isn't Milwaukee, sir. This is Chicago."

Hikeover, "Chicago? Nothing's supposed to be happening in Chicago. We've had zero intel about Chicago. Get me a closer reading."

"Here you are, sir," Todd offers his screen to the general. "There's an unexplained cluster right here," Todd points to a green patch by Lake Michigan.

Animated, Jacob offers, "You know, that's Lincoln Park. Todd speculated it was cars, but it can't be."

Todd responds defensively, "I didn't say for sure it was cars."

"Oh, you said it was a fender bender," accuses Jacob.

"Shush, both of you," Hikeover commands. "There is something happening there. Can we uh, put a drone on it right away?"

"It'll take just a minute or two, Sir. But I'll get you an overhead close-up," Todd offers.

"Yeah, put that in action right now." The general asserts his authority and while Todd turns to take care of the order the General looks straight at Jacob Charles and hisses," And you, you keep your goddamn feet off the desk." Jacob cringes then looks up at the camera in the corner of his cubicle. He's painfully aware that while watching other people, he is being watched. The general turns back to Marcher, "Are there any uh, Hajiis or mosques or temples in the area? You get me a printout," the General barks again, "Also, churches. We can't afford to fuck up. We've missed the last two mosque attacks. I wish those towel heads would keep in their own fucking country. It'd make things a lot simpler."

"I'll get the intel right away," Todd responds.

Jacob offers timidly, "The location. Lincoln Park, sir. It's where the police riot..."

"Police riot?" Hikeover twitches, "What the hell are you talking about, police riot?"

"Back in 1968, the chaos at the August convention. Democratic convention. Chicago, sir. You remember..."

Todd squeals, "Look sir, Grant Park. More activity."

"What the hell, where's the drone? Where's Grant Park?" snaps Hikeover.

Jacob practically jumps out of his chair, "Soldiers Field. Look, hundreds of... what the hell?"

A drone kicks in with a clear overhead picture.

"Bicycles, they're bicycles!" Todd shrieks triumphantly.

"Oh, it's a critical mass," tops Jacob.

"A what?" the general shakes his head in confusion.

"A critical mass, sir. When cyclists have enough riders that they can take over the streets from cars. It's happening right now in Chicago," explains Todd.

"Oh, that has to be illegal," the general croaks, "I mean, come on. Do they have a permit?"

Todd offers condescendingly, "Not to worry sir. They'll just ride around for a few hours before they play out. Angry motorists will honk at them and there'll be a few incidents of road rage and then it will be over."

"Are you sure?" the general doubts.

"Yes sir. I've seen several of them before," says Jacob, "there was one at the New York Republican convention in 2004. My uncle took part."

"Yeah," says Todd, "that's right. They threw a big net on the top of hundreds of riders."

"What? Who threw a net?" the general's confused.

"The cops," explains Jacob.

General Hikeover wonders, "Do we have that many nets ready? I mean, that looks like a lot of riders."

"I suggest, sir, that we just let them ride it out. What harm can come of it?" Todd has regained his composure.

"I agree," nods Jacob, "they're generally a peaceful group. We'll check out the overhead pictures, get some closeups, make sure they're not packing weapons, and then, uh, we'll track them for a little while before they tire..."

Suddenly, a loud, ear-piercing alarm goes off, "BBRRRRRRRRRR!!!!"

The general looks like he's been hit on the side of the head. He holds his temples, "Oh, God, the noise, the noise."

Todd and Jacob shout simultaneously, "Code Red, Code Red." A giant screen drops down on the wall behind the cubicles. All eyes are fixed on the map of the United States. There's activity in Chicago, but what grabs everyone's attention is a huge swath of movement in Ohio.

Jacob shouts, "Just south of Cincinnati on the river. Hundreds of what? Boats. What the hell... boats?"

"Yes," screams Todd, "It's a flotilla!"

"A flotilla?" the General's flabbergasted, "I don't get it."

End of Chapter 1

Colonial Policy

Chapter 2
The Flotilla

Sunday, July 26th

Hundreds of boats, rafts, make-shift floaters, dinghies, inner-tubes-enter the Ohio River south of Cincinnati just past 8AM on this Sunday Midwest morning. Bathed in sunshine a couple of folks even sit astride logs paddling, laughing and rolling along with the flow of the current towards their destination-Louisville, Kentucky. On the northside and the southside riverbanks musicians play their instruments and crowds of onlookers shout encouragement. "*Arriba, Arriba, Andale, Vamanos!*" The invigorating strains of "*Venceramos*"(We Will Win, We Will Win") ring out across the water. Scores of cars on access roads on both sides of the river honk their horns signaling allegiance. Some curious onlookers wonder what in the heck is the spectacle they are witness to. This looks like the Dunkirk evacuation or D-Day. It's neither. It is July 26th and the festive mood commemorates the Cuban Revolution when the people of that tiny island rose up against colonialism perpetrated by the Goliath to the north. What makes the 26th of July such a seminally important day in history is that it symbolically represents the indigenous peoples of Central and South America throwing off the yolk of oppression after 500 years of humiliation and enslavement.

The narrative espoused by the bully to the north is that their hero Christopher Columbus brought civilization to these heathens. He was a savior planting a Christian cross into the soil of a Caribbean island proclaiming ownership by way of a "doctrine of discovery". The reality is, of course, completely different. The natives naively welcomed the disease-ridden marauders seeking a metal-gold-that these pirates worshipped. Though in reality no more precious than any other rock or seashell this metal induced these pock-marked brutes into paroxysms of violence. Mad with greed they slashed and burned in search of a motherlode. To them, vast quantities of gold symbolized power in their warped, war-mad, class-culture. Columbus was not a lone adventurer. He had competitors who rushed to soak up the infinite riches of the New World-perhaps the most sought after natural resource-slave labor! Hernan Cortez led his Spanish conquistadors further West to conquer and enslave still more indigenous peoples. For the following three hundred years more and more conquistadors continued the enslavement of natives for generation after generation. They raped the people and the land we know as Mexico. The Spaniards reign of terror abruptly ended when a young country known as the United States only a half century after its formation provoked a war with the Mexican government and its people. The U.S.'s slave-holding aristocracy wanted to expand their territory. Then President Polk, himself a slave-holder, whipped up his people into a frenzy. War fever swept the American States. Abraham Lincoln early in his political career was one of the few sane voices who saw this for what is was-a nakedly aggressive land grab. Clearly the aggressors, the Americans easily won the barely contested war and forced the signing of a treaty that humiliated the Mexican people. The Treaty of Guadalupe Hildago. Ah, the treaty! Such a lopsided document could hardly find an equal except perhaps in treaties that the American government made and broke with the native Indians in the North. For a measly amount of cash, 15 million dollars, the USA confiscated half of the country of Mexico including all of today's California, Arizona, New Mexico and parts of Utah and Colorado. The land-hungry gringos were merely the mirror image of the gold-hungry conquistadores. And soon the Yankees added one more earthly element for which to go mad-black gold, i.e. oil. The Yanks mantra instead of the "doctrine of discovery" was called "manifest destiny" (same game, different name). O, yes, these crackers claimed divine right. They were listening to god, they were. He(of course it was a "him") spoke directly to them. Conquer, control, and, above all of these sacred commandments-obey authority! The Mexican people still reel today from the consequences of this divisive treaty of Guadalupe Hildago. Think about it in context. 1848 is only about two average lifetimes ago. According to Einstein that's a relatively short time. So, naturally, more and more indigenous voices started asking, "Whose authority?" And that's what happened in Cuba in the 1950s. A small band of *companeros* watched as an American criminal enterprise, the CIA, hired a public relations firm owned by Edward Bernays, nephew of Sigmund Freud. The Cubans witnessed how the CIA led a campaign against their Latin neighbor Guatemala to smear and destabilize the popularly elected soldier turned politician Jacabo Arbenz. Bernays used the "communist" trope and equally fake "domino theory" to scare the populace. Time-tested, this formula of fearmongering worked yet again. Numerous other regime change incidents preceded and followed the Guatemalan debacle-Puerto Rico, Grenada, Chile, Nicaragua, Honduras, El Salvador right up to today's latest news-Venezuela. The architects or rather the puppets of the architects of these violent fascist coups were trained at Fort Benning, Georgia-home of the torture-loving School of the Americas. Latino men were trained there as secret police. They learned how to intimidate and dominate along with the delicate skill of running death squads. They were taught the betrayal of their fellow countrymen and even their own families. Today's migration is a direct result and natural result of these polices. Of course, the talking head neo-liberals and neo-conservatives who pepper the corporate airwaves rarely if ever mention these brutal policies. They don't want the true historical narrative exposed. How economic hitmen are sent by the CIA not to spread democracy but to destabilize countries. And, how the privately owned Federal Reserve Bank spawns institutions like the World Bank and the International Monetary Fund which forces countries into crippling debt. How multi-national corporations like United Fruit manipulate the politics of counties so they can usurp the natural resources for the benefit of their shareholders. They own huge swaths of land, communications systems(including newspapers) and railroads. Indigenous families are forced off what should be their land and shuffled off into cities where jobs are scarce. The insane and failed Drug War has festered for decades and fostered violent drug cartels. Where can a family go to survive? How can a mother or a father protect their family in such a chaotic environment? Add an even greater hardship-drought followed by famine-who wouldn't migrate in whatever direction there might be a safe haven? So, don't dare rush to judgment of a family fleeing the chaos perpetrated by the policies of the U.S. government in partnership with the huge multi-national conglomerates.

The flotilla launched on this historic July day is comprised of hospital workers, hotel workers, kitchen staff, and domestics who do the ironing and laundry of the well-to-do and act as nannies to their children. These humble workers are the backbone of the American economy so are owed our respect. These brave souls, in spite of the risk of deportation, have joined the force of the people as they head down the Ohio River. They demand dignity. These are a proud people and tired of living in the shadows as second class citizens. They feel compelled to challenge the system that's enslaving them and threatening them with a Gestapo-like police force known as I.C.E.

"We did it," gushes Caroline. "We sure as hell did!" enthuses DaNeeda. Caroline Omar-Gomez and DaNeeda Sanchez hug each in an embrace that takes their breaths away. Tears stream down their cheeks. "When you assured me six months ago I thought you might be loco, loco, loco." DaNeeda laughs and cries. Caroline and DaNeeda are the two organizers who diligently worked for over a year to not only make this happen but also keep it under the radar until today's triumphant launch. They had met and bonded at an Arizona I.C.E detention center where they both had gone to pick up the remains of an asylum-seeking family member who had died on the treacherous desert crossing. Bonding as only two sisters can bond through the agony of losing a loved one they vowed to each other to seek vengeance, redress and reparations. They stand erect and sing out on the stern of their craft which they have named "*Si Se Pueda*". Next to them on a pontoon boat is a full mariachi band complete with a trumpet, saxophone, two violins and a guitar. When the troubadours finish with the inspiring words and music of "*Venceramos*" they segue right into Woody Guthrie's popular folk song "This Land is My Land". The flotilla heads toward Louisville to demand the American government end their two hundred year long reign of terror.

* *

The internet hums with activity. Just a couple of days after the opening ceremonies of the Olympics in Tokyo, Japan folks are glued to their television sets rooting for their favorite competitors. Trending in real time sporadic notices are posted with news of the flotilla and the critical mass bike riders who, by the way, have left Chicago and have already penetrated several miles deep into Indiana. The cyclists appear to have been vigorously trained. When they pass a mall overlooking the freeway individual bikers peel off the mass and deliver card-sized handouts of the fifty notions for all nations. Their mission is to win the hearts and minds of the businesses and shoppers in the mall. They have been instructed to "invite, not fight". And, the cyclists have coordinated with scores of activists who gather at the malls as "flash mobs" where they break into song throughout large box stores like Macy's, Nordstrom's, Target, Kohl's and, of course, Walmart's. They sing "We Shall Overcome" and "Blowing In The Wind". Their aim is to wake the shoppers up from their soporific stupor of mindless consumerism in which they are entrapped. The message..."Change or Stay Chained". And, the even more urgent message the cyclists and the flash mob activists are trying to convey is for people in cities around the world to figure out a way to stop these daily rush hour traffic jams that throw off tons of carbon into our delicate atmosphere. Surely, if humans can come together and send a man to the moon they can collectively figure out how to regulate traffic. The effort needs to be made now, not next year but next week at the Louisville Jubilee great gathering. No more naysaying. No more hate. Let the haters stew in their own hate. Life is too short. This is a movement about the love of the earth, the love of life.

* *

Back at the NSA New York headquarters General Hikeover is once again barking out orders. Momentarily stunned by the double whammy of a Critical Mass cyclists and the Ohio River flotilla he struggled to regain his military composure. Never in all the mock invasions and the defensive drills had he or any of his peers ever envisioned a flotilla. Drones have now been dispatched to the river and Hikeover shouts into his cell phone at the Governor of Indiana, "I don't care if they have a permit. Revoke it. So many bikes on a freeway has to be illegal. Arrest them." And, as an afterthought, "Throw nets over them." The general punches his phone. Timidly Jacob Charles approaches, "What, Jacob?" the general huffs. "Sir," Jacob stammers, "on the upper left hand of the monitor...that's our own CCTV downstairs in the lobby. General Hikeover glares at the screen. His jaw drops, "That's here?

Downstairs?" Jacob nods. Outside the entrance of the downtown NYC building Reverend Willy and his thirty-strong singing choir have gathered to protest NSA spying on the citizens of the United States. A charismatic leader always messaging the need to protect mother earth, Reverend Willy is one of the most effective environmental activists in the country if not the world. His schtick is to dress in an all-white suit with a clerical collar. He preaches fire and brimstone like a cliché Southern Baptist preacher. But, his message is not one of humble obedience to some higher authority, no, his message loudly and clearly states that he is going to protect the earth. And, he has put his body at risk numerous times doggedly chaining himself to bull dozers, logging trucks and challenging pipeline builders and natural gas frackers wherever he can find them. Media savvy, Reverend Willy looks into the CCTV camera and booms, "Get thee back, Satan. We have no sympathy for the devil. Shame on ye, ye corporate prostitutes and media presstitutes. Our democracy is not for sale. We are here to protect mother earth-earthaleujah!"

"Arrest them, now,' shouts Hikeover. "Invoke national security. Get them the hell outta here." He turns to Jacob accusingly, "Somebody leaked. How the fuck do they know we're in here?" He mumbles almost to himself, "We need undercovers. Boots on the ground." Todd Marcher winks at Jacob and whispers almost gleefully out of earshot of the general, "And, fins in the water!" Jacob's eyebrows shoot up an inch. He's terrified the general might have heard. "Marcher," screams the general, "Call an emergency meeting in the theatre. Now. Haste-poste-haste." "Yes, Sir," Todd clicks his heels. "Jacob, I want you to get word to our undercover unit to infiltrate, now. On the river and on the freeway. Get close to the leaders. Stick on them like stink on shit. We have to find out who's behind this insurrection. Why are you still standing here? Quick. Quick. Go. Now, double time. No, no, wait," the general grabs Jacob's arm and pulls him close. He furtively surveils the room to make sure no one listens, then whispers, "Jacob, bring me back an encrypted phone!"

End of Chapter 2

> ### *Bhopal, India*
> *December 3, 1984*
>
> *Bhopal was home to around 800,000 people. Around 3,000 died immediately. Another 4,000 to 7,000 died in the next few days, many in horrible agony. According to Amenity International another 15,000 died years later from cancer, tuberculosis, gynecological diseases and other illnesses. In the early 2000s 10 to 15 people died from poison-related diseases every month. Tens of thousands suffered from blindness and ulcers. As of 2004, an estimated 100,000 people were disabled or living with chronic pain.*
>
> *Union Carbide an American company, set up the Bhopal factory in 1980 to produce the powerful pesticide Sevin and "help the country's agricultural sector increase its productivity and contribute more significantly to meeting the food needs of one of the world's most heavily populated regions."*
>
> *The MIC gas that did the damage was used to make pesticides. Twenty-seven tons of it leaked out of a large storage tank after an explosion and drifted over Bhopal neighborhoods near the factory while people were sleeping. People awoke gasping and choking on their own body fluids. The tank was 90 percent full even though safety regulations s specified it to never be more than half full. At the Union Carbide facility in West Virginia MIC is kept in small concentrations to minimize the risk.*

Chapter 3
The Dover Dirge

July 26th, Dover, Delaware

"The worms crawl in, the worms crawl out, the worms crawl all over your mouth and snout."

A shiny black Cadillac hearse inches out from a downtown Dover parking garage. Walking alongside several men dressed in black business suits. This is their mourning attire. These men are known as the "Yes Men" and have carried out over the years several successful hoaxes. Perhaps their most notorious caper was to get the huge multi-national corporation, Union Carbide, admit to their negligence in the Bhopal, India chemical pesticide spill that caused thousands of horrific deaths. Today the Yes Men have a different mission. Accompanied by scores of activists they transport a casket filled with corporate documents that reveal crimes of money laundering and corruption at the very core of several notable "family friendly" businesses like Wells Fargo, Volkswagen, etc... These are smoking guns to the fraud perpetuated on the public. The documents have been supplied by an anonymous whistleblower who pilfered them from a white shoe Dover law firm. Because whistleblowers usually become targets instead of heroes he or she will remain in the shadows for now. The skeletons are all here in this casket-proof of collusion between banks and drug cartels, tax dodges cheating honest taxpayers out of billions of dollars.

Walking behind the hearse are several elegantly dressed ladies with exaggeratedly long cigarette holders and their gentlemen escorts in tuxedos and top hats. These are the resurrected "Billionaires For Bush". A bus waits for the black limousine at a curb outside the traffic structure. They will follow the hearse all the way to Washington D.C. where copies of the documents will be dropped off, first at the FBI offices, then the Internal Revenue Service where demands for action will be publicized. Of course, they will take a slow ride down K Street where they will be handing out to corporate lobbyists the card-sized fifty notions for all nations. Boarding the bus in Dover are several activists carrying signs which they will be displaying in D.C. "Thank you Chelsea Manning", "Free Julian Assange", "We miss you Edward Snowden", "Shame on GAFA!" which refers to the relatively young hugely profitable companies Google, Amazon, Facebook and Apple. The papers in this casket are cold, hard evidence that these companies are fleecing the public with complex tax dodges. Their legal departments protest(too much) that what they do is legal but everybody knows the loopholes in the tax codes are written by lawmakers who are paid for with hefty campaign donations. It's not exactly a well-kept secret. *Cui bono?* Who benefits? Follow the money. The dots are easily connected. As the group of demonstrators tuck their placards into the bus luggage compartment one of the placards falls onto the street. A short stocky fellow picks it up and reads its one word message out loud, which says it all..."TRANSPARENCY!!!"

* *

In Louisville, Code Purple's Meredith Ann Baker, who has already been dubbed "Queen Mab" by local media, strikes deal after deal with businesses in the greater metropolitan area. Just now she's mingling with the city's big wigs in the board room of the Southern Comfort Country Club. Meredith has endeared herself to the mayor, Craig Trout, and his wife, Marly. The three have become besties. Craig has had the fortitude to fight back against an overwhelming onslaught from the Governor who has been demanding the Mayor close down the city rather than host a gathering of "freaks and geeks", i.e., anybody who doesn't hold the archaic political opinions of the Republican governor. To his everlasting credit, the Mayor has not given in to the bullying tactics. Besides, as a successful entrepreneur himself, Craig's aware that next week's exhibition will be a bonanza for local businesses. The hotels for miles around are solidly booked for the next couple of weeks. So overloaded are the hotels and motels Meredith has asked for this meeting at the country club with the board members. At first, her request to have tents erected on the golf course was met with guffaws, derision, amazement and laugh out loud rejection. But, because in her short time in the city Meredith has established a reputation for integrity, the elders have given her a chance to lobby for her proposal. The Southern Comfort Country Club has a unique history in the annals of private clubs throughout the country. It's been written about in scores of opinion pieces across the political spectrum. Within the past decade the club integrated after a century of "white-only" membership. Young Louisville progressive businessmen and women voted themselves onto the board of directors and radically changed the club. What had been a stuffy old white man's racist conclave has transformed into a hip, Louisville multi-cultural hotspot. Upbeat dances open to the public are held two or three times per month. The board hired as chef Massoud Hussan a connoisseur of Middle Eastern food. His specialty is Iranian cuisine. He's become a local celebrity with his own televised cooking show.

Meredith continues addressing the board around noon on Sunday the 26th, "We pledge to honor the land and leave your grounds at least in as good shape as they are now, maybe even better. Bobby McGrath, a recognized world expert on grasses, soil and plants will supervise the effort." Bobby, from the back of the room tips his baseball cap.

Board member Pete Womack interjects, "Who's going to pay for all this...the water bill, the port-o-potties...?"

"Of course," Meredith patiently answers, "your club will incur no out of pocket costs. The Jubilee collective will foot all bills..." Bobby checks in from the back, "We will replace and renew every trampled blade of grass."

Someone asks about protecting the greens. Bobby assures him, "The greens will be clearly marked by yellow tape. They will be no-go zones and patrolled by fellow naturalists."

"Look," Meredith retakes the talking stick, "we're well aware there might be agent provocateurs mingling within our midst anytime over the next few weeks. We've dealt with them many times before. They are a problem. That's why we've taken out a one hundred thousand dollar insurance policy and given your club a twenty thousand dollar retainer."

Mayor Trout follows, "You see, Pete, they're good for business. I told'ya."

Another board member, Charlie Carpenter, genuinely concerned about the stewardship of his beloved club, asks plaintively, "Hey, I like what you and your colleagues are trying to do, Meredith. I'm all for it, I really am, but I'm having trouble endorsing this plan. Everybody knows we humans have a tendency, hell a proclivity, to trash environments. And, accidents happen even without the threat of agent provocateurs. Come on, this is way too risky."

"Carp," the mayor offers, "I felt the same way. I laughed at the idea at first. But then Marly and I thought about it. We weighed the importance of the upcoming conference discussions about climate change and concluded the juice is worth the squeeze."

"I don't know," Carp's not sure, "I'm having trouble picturing tents along the fourteenth fairway." Spike Flannery, board member and golfing buddy pipes up, "You won't even notice them, Carp. With your slice you're always in the rough on that hole!" There's general laughter that lightens the atmosphere. The board seems to be siding with Meredith's heartfelt plea. Carp sighs and seems to finalize in favor of Meredith, "All right, I guess so."

The meeting's adjourned with an agreement for Meredith and McGrath to meet with the club's attorneys to draw up a contract that will deal with particulars of the soon to be Southern Comfort tent city. Lydia Baez has been taking notes. She cuts off Meredith who's about to exit. "Got a minute, Meredith?"

"Yeh, sure. What's up?"

"The Jubilee Collective. First I heard of'em? Who are they?" Lydia, obviously a little suspicious.

"We have no secrets. I'll give you a list of our donors. Lots of folks who have made money in our wide open economy realize we need to curb certain industrial practices that are destroying our planet faster than it can replenish itself. And, these practices have us cascading towards chaos. We need to deal with these issues now, Lydia. That's what you had me on your show to explain."

"Will you put me in touch with some of your wealthy donors?" asks Lydia.

"Sure," says Meredith. "Come on, ride with me back to the gardens. You can call anyone of them from my car. Bobby's already on his bike and challenged me to a race back."

* *

At the New York City National Security headquarters General Hikeover blurts out, Dover, Delaware? What the fuck? Is this connected?"

"Can't tell for sure," says Todd squinting into his screen. "We've got a drone overhead."

"Oh, look," butts in Jacob. "The hearse is moving towards the street. There's a bus by the curb waiting."

The general mutters to himself barely audible, "We need undercovers. Where the hell are they?"

End of Chapter 3.

Tombs in the Desert

Chapter 4
"Old Man River"

Sunday, July 26th

Navigating the Ohio River can be precarious. There are all sorts of tricks that only experience can master. Soon after the flotilla launch several of the more unstable skiffs capsize and disappointed folks have to be fished out of the water. Caroline and DaNeeda watch nervously as rescue missions are carried out skillfully. In spite of the danger the mood remains festive and the sun continues to shine. Turning to DaNeeda, Caroline raises her fist to the sky, "This is for you, Ramon," she shouts out at the top of her lungs. DaNeeda knows only too well she's referring to her brother who died on the Arizona desert abandoned by the guide, the coyote, just like DaNeeda's Tia Emily. Both relatives came within miles of their destination when a border patrol helicopter flew over and scared the person they had paid to lead them safely across the desert. He took with him all the remaining water. One can only imagine the panic and then the slow agonizing drift into unconsciousness with the vultures circling.

Watching a rescue on the river Caroline shakes her head, "We warned people about climbing into leaky boats. We begged them to carefully check their crafts before entering the water." DaNeeda captures the moment on her cell phone camera. "I think everybody's back on board. Here, take a look. The last swimmer's okay." She hands her phone over. Caroline gazes at the screen, "I wish those macho hot dogs riding on the logs would get onto someone's boat. They are a disaster waiting to happen," then excitedly, "Oh, look. We've already made the news."

* *

In Dover, Delaware the hearse, followed by the bus, has left downtown. They both have their headlights on in a mock funeral procession. The bus vibrates with energy. A little fireplug of a guy, Dexter Holloway, jumps up and down in the aisle like a pogo stick. "Come on people, sing it loud and sing it clear. Pookie, can't you get some more noise out of the squeeze box?" The colorfully clad blonde standing by the front seat of the bus goes by the single moniker-Pookie. For years she's been a crowd favorite whenever or wherever she's able to find a crowd. She always packs her accordion and given the slightest opening she breaks into song like a lovebird charming a mate. Sitting beside her a young man with tattoos all over his upper body begins to scratch his hands on a washboard. Pookie sways into her signature Zydeco song, *Je Suis Comme Ca."* Quickly the atmosphere lights up as she punches out a lively tune on her keyboard. Dexter charges up and down the aisle passing out Mardi Gras beads and Hawaiian leis. Giddy with excitement he hugs one rider after another. Finally, exhausted he drops next to his dear friend Schotzy who sits in the back of the bus. Dexter's head plops down onto her lap. She strokes his sweaty brow and he coos like a dove. Without Schotzy Dexter would have crashed and burned years ago. She's just about the only person who can keep his manic behavior in check. In truth, though, they are co-dependent. Schotzy's almost completely blind from glaucoma and cataracts. Dexter operates as her seeing eye dog. They met in Tijuana. Schotzy had worked for many years in Hollywood where she reigned as the uncrowned "queen of the soaps" a title give her by industry cognoscenti. She had been the Girl Friday for many male producers at a time when women had to remain in the shadows in order to survive. A master storyteller she oversaw what's known in soap opera lingo as "the bible" behind the scenes. She said when it was time for an evil twin to return from the dead or how a male heir was switched at birth. This was and is the fodder of the soap operas that are watched by millions. Unhappy as a neglected child Schotzy escaped her misery by creating a wonderful fantasy world but she had also developed an eating disorder that caused her to become severely overweight. This only led to more isolation. And, even though she was highly sought after in Hollywood for her talent, she was never truly comfortable in that body shaming culture where only the slim are beautiful. Finally she said, "enough" to the male-dominated, ego-driven Holy Woods and found a much more satisfying career as a counselor to refugees on the Mexican border. And, that's how she met Dexter who needed someone to bail him out of the Mexican pokey after a week-long binge. He was absolutely penniless so she provided him a place to stay just as her eyesight was rapidly deteriorating. Thus a bond was formed. He took care of her and she took care of him. Always rooting for the underdog, it was her idea to lend her talent where it might be useful in going over the cache of documents. Dexter would read the documents aloud, Schotzy would interpret them. Happier now than she had ever been, she sits back contentedly as the bus rocks towards Washington D.C., the devil's playground.

* *

In New York City the heads of every National Security department gather in the theatre on the 24th floor. This is their so-called war room. General Hikeover paces back and forth in front of a large spotlighted map of the United States. He brandishes a wooden pointer like it's a medieval sword. There are at least a score of uniformed elderly white men all of whom are loaded down with various medals signifying who knows what? They listen attentively. "We know where the targets are headed," Hikeover slams the pointer squarely on Louisville. "The kick-off event is next Saturday, we've been able to learn that much from our sources. We'll know a lot more presently. But this much I can tell you. We are in a crisis mode. Our national security is at stake!" The general relishes his role as lead actor with supporting roles played by a slew of other generals, major-generals, colonels, lieutenant-colonels and even an admiral dressed in his all-white dress uniform. All nod somberly. "I want each of you to man your stations for the next twelve hours as we work our way through this code red crisis. We have to be alert for a cyber invasion. Most likely coming from the Chinese or the Russians." "Or the Iranians, " one of the officers suggests. ""Yes, yes, to be sure," agrees Hikeover, "I want to know about any and all the bleeps on your radar screens. And, monitor your drones. Admiral Zimmer..."

"Yes, sir," snaps Zimmer.

"You, of course will oversee the river operation. I expect hourly updates. Gentlemen, keep your earphones on and man your stations. "Sir," the men salute in unison and quick step towards the exit. While the room empties the general signals to his two adjutants. "Todd," the general rasps, "any feedback from the surveillance unit?" "Nothing yet, Sir. But they assured me they would have complete intel on the leaders within 24 hours. They will flush out any foreign influence." "Good, good," the general pats Todd on the shoulder, "We need that. Get back to your station." Todd exits. "Jacob, did you get me what I asked?" "Here, Sir," Jacob takes a cell phone from his pocket and tries giving it to the general. "No, no you keep it. Tonight at precisely 6pm I want you to call this number," Hikeover gives him a slip of paper. "After you've made the call burn the paper. This is top secret. Do you understand?" I hear you loud and clear, Sir," Jacob assures the general. "Young lad, you are about to be part of history. If there's one man in this nation who can singlehandedly abort this insurrection he will answer our call." "Sir?" Jacob's not sure how to respond. The general says reverently, "You will be creating a back channel with Derrick Quince."

"Derrick Quince!!" repeats Jacob, "the Darkwater CEO?"

The general nods slowly up and down, "Absolute secrecy. Tell him I need him here ASAP!"

* *

Back at "the gardens" Meredith engages Marly, the Mayor's wife, "We sure can use the help, thanks. Would you feel comfortable greeting some of the musicians on their arrival and coordinating their lodging?"

Marly smiles, "You mean I might get to meet the great Willy Nelson?"

"Yep, he'll be coming in for the Saturday night finale at Churchhill Downs," assures Meredith.

"Super. Count on me." Marly loves Country & Western.

Meredith on a different tack confides, "You know, when that board member Carp raised doubts about our ability to keep your club trash free I wanted to invite him and the other members to the workshop on Monsanto and pesticides. Let them see who's really trashing the fairways and greens. All that stuff your guys are drenching into the soil eventually seeps into the groundwater."

"There's still time to tell'em," says Marly. "When is the workshop? I'd like to go. I'm in my garden hours at a time."

"Wednesday the fifth, I think," Meredith checks her cell phone, "Yeh, late afternoon."

Marly offers, "We all need to learn more about the adverse effect of pesticides on the environment. We have to start growing more naturally. And golf courses, yikes, they are the elephant in the room.

Meredith relieved, "I'm glad you said it first.

End of Chapter 4

Dancing By Fire

"Wetiko"

Chapter 5
Dexter's Vision

July 26th

Dover, Delaware is only sixty or so miles from Annapolis, Maryland, home of the Naval Academy. In just over an hour the caravan of the hearse and the bus reach their first stop at the front entrance to the Academy. Dexter's first off the bus and he carries his bull horn, "Who do you work for, swabbies?" he blares in front of the guard shack to no one in particular. Dex bounces over to the hearse parked by the curb and points, "In this black limousine are your get-out-of-service permits. You are risking your lives for a bunch of crooks who don't care a hoot for you. Quit following orders from megalomaniacs who want to profit from perpetual war. The papers inside tell the whole truth and nothing but the truth, so help me, so help you." Several military police officers approach. Dexter cowers in mock fear. "Don't lock me up, please, Mr. Policemen. And, Mrs. Policewoman, sorry, I didn't notice you. I'm not crazy. Just trying to save some young lives."

The lead officer politely tells Dexter, "Sir, the bus and limo have to move. This is a military compound and the entrance has to be clear at all times."

"Aye, aye, Captain," Dexter salutes and clicks his heals. "Just stopped by to say hello." He turns to the limo driver, bus driver and passengers and barks into his bull horn, "The brass says we're not welcome. Outta here, my peeps. D.C here we come but first a rendezvous with our confreres at Grady's Farm!"

* *

Critical Mass Bikers are popping up everywhere. In the North, the East, the West, the South. N>E>W>S=NEWS. Local radio and television stations are on the case. In Tennessee there's a breaking report of one hundred Elvis impersonators on bicycles who have left from the front of Graceland. They are on their way to Louisville with a pit stop scheduled in Nashville at the Grand Ol' Opry where they will perform an ensemble of Jose Marti's "Guantanamera"-the Cuban revolutionary song. After all, they're leaving on the 26th of July though they won't sing until the following day. When a local anchor hears about the impersonators plan to sing the Cuban anthem at the iconic Grand Ol' Opry she blurts out off-script, "America's role in colonialism is clearly being challenged."

Another critical mass of cyclists launches from Kansas City, Missouri-the "show-me" state. They sport placards that say, "We are fugitive wage slaves" and "No more compromise!" These are allusions to the failed 1820 legislation, The Missouri Compromise.

A huge number of riders have amassed outside of Oklahoma City bearing placards like "Put McVeigh in Play", and "O.K. Bombing not Okay!" Traffic on Highway 44 stands still as several indigenous riders join up carrying their placards one of which proclaims, "Jubilee 2020, Trail of Joy!"

* *

General Hikeover sits behind his desk in his office at the New York NSA headquarters. Clearly feeling the heat he's addressing a handful of section heads, "There is no possible way that this a spontaneous eruption. This took planning. It's imperative we pinpoint which of our enemies is behind this outrage. Who are the leaders of this uprising and what country is financing them."

Admiral Zimmer interjects, "We've been tracking several so-called climate action groups over the past few years. We call them eco-terrorists."

Another three star general chimes in, "The movement gained prominence a couple of years ago when the Lakota Sioux Indians demonstrated against a pipeline that encroached on their land."

"Standing Rock," chips in a junior officer, "Mi Wiconi."

"Me what?" demands Hikeover.

"Mi Wiconi, sir. Water is life." the young officer speaks almost reverently.

"Oh, Jesus," the general spits out, "A fucking bunch of bleeding hearts."

* *

Crowds are stretched for miles along both banks of the Ohio River cheering the flotilla as it floats by. Thankfully, the weather holds. Every kind of noisemaker blasts across the water. Several blue grass groups pluck on their banjos in the bright sunshine. Still in the lead craft Caroline and DaNeeda surveil their handywork. They hug each other. Caroline sighs, "Who would've believed we would get this kind of reception?"

Her dear friend DaNeeda with tears drenching her cheeks sobs, "Americans are good people. They care. They understand."

* *

Meredith Ann Baker confers with Bobby McGrath, "Do you believe I just got a call from the Democratic Party. They want us to call off the entire Jubilee. Cancel the whole shebang after all the frigging work we've done!"

Animated, McGrath offers, "We are not about political compromise. The issues we will be addressing are too critical. We need immediate solutions. We can't kick any cans down the road so some asshole billionaire and his buddies can continue to rape our planet. We will have our exposition of possibilities, come hell or highwater."

"The highwater will come first, then the hell if we don't take care of business," Meredith shrugs, "I'm not even taking their calls anymore.

"A waste of time," agrees McGrath.

"But," Queen Mab informs McGrath, "I've invited a coalition of Democratic hopefuls. Most of them were shut out of the DNC-too radical. They'll hold a five hour caucus on Thursday, August 6th."

"Great," claps McGrath, "We want to hear from them."

* *

The sunset from the hillside of Grady's Farm in the Maryland backwoods shimmers across the fields. It's only called a farm. Grady bought the land years ago with the dream of retiring here to raise chickens, goats and a few pigs. He called it his "forty acres and a mule". But, Grady ran out of time on realizing his dream so when he heard that the Dover caravan needed a rest stop he eagerly offered his "farm". He even donated three port-o-potties towards the effort. As the sun sets several activists clear brush away and prepare a large fire pit. In just a few minutes the sun will drop behind the hills and the air will cool. Dexter leads Schotzy to a padded recliner that he carries with them wherever they travel. Someone cautions not to get too close as the flames will soon be lapping at the sky. Dexter is Schotzy's official caretaker. In truth though, Schotzy is Dexter's keeper. She's his therapy dog and keeps his manic behavior somewhat in balance. Pookie doesn't even wait for the fire to start. She kicks into her Irish repertoire. Several flutes and a fiddle join in. She'll hold back only a wee bit for now. She'll play "Danny Boy" later when the fire blazes.

* *

The tillerman eases the lead craft towards the western bank of the Ohio. Caroline Omar Gomez high-fives DaNeeda, "Can you fucking believe it? We did it. We pulled off the greatest July 26th celebration ever."

"Hands down, the greatest," claps DaNeeda. "I sure had my doubts. Just a month ago when I.C.E raided the poultry factory I thought we were toast."

"Yeh, those heartless bastards. We lost a lot of hardworking people who would have been here by our side. But we soldiered on and we have created a publicity coup like no other," beams Caroline.

Waving her cell phone DaNeeda states victoriously, "We're making headlines across the country.

* *

As a matter of record, as they congratulated each other CNN continues their live feeds to Times Square. The bleachers, now, are packed to the gills. Lots of tourists stand in the streets gaping at the giant screen. They are no longer focused so much on the Olympics as on the Bikers. It's just been announced that a Puerto Rican Critical Mass and a Gay Pride Critical Mass have within the last hour left the greater New York area heading South. The competitive juices are flowing. They've placed a large bet on who will reach Louisville first. The excitement easily matches that of the Olympics. The spectators in the stands and on the streets are bingeing on the energy and loving it.

* *

After getting Schotzy comfortably seated in her cushy lounge chair, Dexter hops up and begins barking directions at a couple of young men prepping the bond fire. After just a minute, one of the youngsters in his early 20s stops what he is doing and looks squarely at Dexter, "Look, Pops, cool your jets. You are going to have to stand back." Dexter's all set to mix it up, however inappropriately. In the nick of time Schotzy calls out in a deep voice, "Dexter Holloway, come over here. I need your help for just a moment." Like a puppy Dexter obeys. "What do you need, Mama?" Schotzy, in no way showing disrespect for Dexter's energy, tells him in a matter of fact, "I need to know the itinerary for tomorrow when we get to D.C." She distracts him from a potential stupid confrontation.

"I can't get into it right now, I'll tell you later," pants Dexter, "I just swallowed a handful of schrooms and they're starting to kick in."

"Oh, dear," sighs Schotzy. Dexter sits down beside her shivering. She puts her arm around him. There's a loud whoosh as the bond fire is lit.

The volunteers who built this fire must have graduated from Burning Man. The flames instantly shoot for the sky. Shooting stars are everywhere. For a moment the musicians halt and silently gaze in awe into the sparkling heavens. Around the campfire there's a shared vision of our spectacular universe.

"Oh, boy," exudes Dexter. He gazes into the flames.

"Tell me, Dex," Schotzy can't hide her eagerness to share a contact high, "Tell me every detail."

"Oh, Mama, Mama," Dexter rolls into a slow moan. He stares into the fire, "It's like nothing I've ever seen before. I can see everything at once. Deep, deep into the bowels of our sacred planet. Ohhhhh!" His eyes widen, "Hold me, Mama. Hold me tight. Hug meeeee."

"I'm right here, Dex. I've gottcha," Schotzy reassures Dexter, "Pookie's here."

"There **he** is. Right there, Schotzy. Right in front of me." Dexter tries to squirm out of Schotzy's grip but she holds him tightly.

"Who, Dexter? Who's there? Don't be scared," Schotzy tries to calm her shaking friend.

"Beeazlebub. The Demon!" Dexter's voice falters, "Right in front of me, beckoning. That red devil's trying to pull me into the fire. Don't let him, Schotzy. Please don't let him take me."

"You're staying right here with us, Dexter. We've got your back. Nobody's gonna take you from us," Schotzy tamps down Dexter's naked fear.

Dexter's body shutters and he spasm's before becoming absolutely still. He utters low, slow, and soberly, "Wetiko..., Wetiko..., Wetiko. The virus spreads. D.C. is a hotbed. We all have to be careful." Spent, Dexter buries his head in Schotzy's bosom but before he drifts off into sleep he whispers, "I am you, you are me. You are my creator," Dexter's voice trails off but not before uttering quietly, "We have to be careful...Wetiko!!!"

End of Chapter 5

Rush Hour

Chapter 6
God & Country

Monday, July 27th

On the top floor of the "secret" New York National Security building Derrick Quince kneels in front of an unfurled American flag. General Hikeover's by his side. A small figure of Christ on a cross leans against the flag. They pray in silence. After several moments Derrick begins to quietly chant the rosary after making the sign of the cross, "The apostles creed: Our Father, Hail Mary, Hail Mary, Hail Mary, Glory be..."

Simultaneously, General Hikeover mumbles the Lord's Prayer, "Our Father, who art in heaven, hallowed be Thy name, Thy kingdom come, Thy will be done, on earth as it is in heaven..."

When both have completed their ritual prayers Quince stands erect and wraps the figure of Christ in a velvet cloth and puts it into his brief case. He carefully unhooks the flag from the wall and folds it purposefully.

General Hikeover begins their *tête-à-tête*, "Thank you for coming here, Derrick, on such short notice."

Derrick, in a steady monotone, responds, "I was watching the news when I got the call."

Hikeover- "I knew your father. Great man, really a great man."

Quince- "Thank you, sir."

Hikeover- "We served together in Nam. He was tougher than nails. A leader of men like no other. You must be proud."

Quince- "I am, sir."

Hikeover- "They tried to break him."

Quince- "Sir?"

Hikeover- "We were on patrol in the jungle when the little bastards ambushed us. He was taken captive, held for a week. The rest of us escaped."

Quince- "He would never talk about that ."

Hikeover- "Not even to us. During his debriefing the brass tried to get him to talk. How'd he get away? What'd they do to him? He wouldn't utter a peep. Not a god-damned word. Like I said, hard as steel."

Quince- "Always."

Hikeover- "They tried all the interrogation tricks-good cop, bad cop...nothing-like a mummy."

Quince- "Never showed any emotion-ever."

Hikeover- "He was even threatened with a court martial. But he wouldn't budge. We all assumed he'd been unmercifully tortured."

Quince- "He held it in unto death. Never opened up."

Hikeover- "That was your father, strong, brave, unbreakable. He was our hero."

"Mine, too," Quince concurs.

Hikeover concludes, "Great man, a really, really, great man."

There's a slight awkward pause. Derrick's not completely comfortable talking about his father who he's revered but also feared all his life. He breaks the silence, "What can Darkwater do for you?"

Hikeover- "We have a situation, as you're aware. I need boots on the ground...in several locations. They have to be mobile."

Quince- "We have five thousand superior troops on the ready. Tell me where."

Hikeover- "Not open troops. I need undercovers. No visibility."

Quince- "We are all purpose, sir. T.I.S. Total Intelligence Solutions."

Hikeover- "Good. We need to identify the leaders."

Quince- "Snatch and grab? You want to interrogate?"

Hikeover-"No, no. Just intel, for now. Kidnapping might cause too much blowback. I need deniability."

Quince- "Deniability is built into everything we do."

Hikeover-"You understand that my fingerprints can't be found anywhere!"

"I know that, sir," Derrick reassures the general, "I'm going to personally take command of this action. I'll report back to you within 72 hours."

"Good, this is code red, operate at your discretion. Time is of the essence," Hikeover firmly shakes Derrick's hand. Then he suddenly pulls Quince forward and gives him a bear hug. Fighting back tears, "The country needs you, desperately."

Quince pulls back, "Roger, 10-4, over and out." Derrick salutes.

* *

The Dover bus rumbles slowly behind the hearse. Both still have their lights on but bumper to bumper Beltway traffic makes no special path for them. Lots of stressed out folks prepare for another week heading to jobs they really don't care about except for the paycheck. Who would, given any choice, subject themselves to this mindless routine day after day? Someone likened it to factory assembly line work and coined the phrase, "The conveyor beltway". Dexter sleeps serenely in Schotzy's lap. Pookie peers out her window, frowning, "I can't believe anyone would torture themselves with this collective madness five days a week!"

"And sometimes on weekends," sighs Schotzy, "Cars, cars, cars."

"Doesn't anyone care about the exhaust that's choking us all?" Pookie wonders, "I mean, give me a break. This is going on in every reasonably sized city-not just in America but all over the world!"

Schotzy shrugs, and adds philosophically, "There sure are a lot of elephants in the room that nobody wants to talk about."

"Yeh," replies Pookie, resigned but simmering, "Republican elephants."

"I hope the Democrats kick ass," Schotzy asserts.

"Won't be long now. We'll know in a few months," reminds Pookie.

"If we get out of this traffic jam in time to vote!" says Schotzy, sarcastically. Dexter stirs, lifts his head slightly, "Are we there, yet?" then groans, "Ohhhhh..."

"Go back to sleep, Dex," counsels Schotzy, "another hour at least."

* *

Meredith Ann Baker sits in the back seat of a Louisville black and white squad car. Sheriff Ted Dearborne sits beside her. "I'm here to help you," he says earnestly.

"I'm overwhelmed, Sheriff Dearborne," states Meredith. "This is the last thing I expected. Personal protection from Louisville's finest!"

"The threats are real, Meredith, and please, call me Ted. We've found dozens of internet angry hate talk exchanges directed at you personally."

Meredith resigned, "That goes with the territory. This is nothing new. Ever since I started speaking out against regime change, drones, war, you name it... I've been called some of the most vile things..."

Ted cuts her off, "Well, until we can trace the origins, it's our job to protect you 24/7."

"Hey," shrugs Meredith, "Who am I to object? I'm just having a tough time trying to take it all in. Mayor Trout's been so accommodating. Then his wife volunteers to help co-ordinate with the bands. Now you."

"I take my job seriously, Meredith. Just like Craig takes his. We were both born and raised in this city. We love it here and don't want any crazies hell bent on violence to disrupt the peace. Craig and I go back a long way. We've been friends since kindergarten. As a matter of fact, I dated Marly before he did."

"No joke!" says Meredith still trying to puzzle together what he's telling her.

"We were both Navy seals. Same unit. Trained together and fought side by side, several tours of duty. Iraq and Afghanistan," continues Ted, "When we got out, he finished college and went into politics. I went straight into law enforcement, something I always wanted."

"Well, it's a noble profession if it's on the side of the people," Meredith feels compelled to state her opinion, "but an evil force when used to oppress the will of the people."

"Understood," agrees the sheriff with no hesitation, "When Craig and Marly led the charge to integrate the country club, there was lots of push back and hundreds of threats."

"Push back from the Governor, I'm sure," Meredith watches his reaction.

"Oh, yeah," says Ted, "The governor's a complete and total jerk. He tried to reinstate ten of my officers who I fired for their affiliation with a white nationalist group."

"Really," ponders Meredith. "Right now I'm more than pleasantly surprised. I just never expected this type of support from city officials, particularly law enforcement."

"Craig's right about your bringing business to the city. And the vital issues you'll be discussing need a public forum. By the way, you don't need to worry about Craig buckling to the governor. Never has, never will," assures the sheriff.

"I sure appreciate your telling me all this. And for the protection, too, of course." She pauses, then, hopefully, "I wonder...would you consider taking part in a workshop on law enforcement?"

"My days off are Saturday and Sunday," replies Ted matter of fact.

Meredith quickly glances at her phone, "Perfect. Saturday morning August 8th, 8AM. You'll be a great addition. I warn you ahead of time, the title is: "Demilitarizing Our Police," she cautions.

"Don't worry. I don't like packing all this gear. Neither do my men except for a few hot dogs we'd like to weed out. It alienates us from the folks we should be identifying with. But the weapon manufacturers keep getting their way. Hell, they want us to patrol in their expensive armored cars like we were in an occupied territory. We don't like the pressure that's coming down from above."

Meredith gazes at Ted thoughtfully, "This has been an enlightening and encouraging dialogue. What you've just told me makes this whole Jubilee experience worth the effort." Meredith reaches across the back seat and firmly shakes the Sheriff's hand while looking him square in the eyes, "Thanks, Ted."

* *

Washington Post building, K St., District of Columbia.

Dexter leaps from the bus holding his ever-ready bull horn. "Okay, Woodward and Bernstein, we got the goods," he shouts out to no one in particular. Several employees are still hurrying to their offices. A young female security guard, not sure what to make of Dex speaks into her shoulder mic and moves towards him slowly. "We're just here to deliver the smoking guns," Dexter sees that she has reacted instinctively to the word "guns". He steps back exhibiting non-aggressiveness. "Metaphorically, m'am, metaphorically. This young man here just wants to deliver this box of <u>papers</u> to the front desk." Somewhat relieved but still cautious she asks to look into the box before the young volunteer can take it inside. She's joined by several of her colleagues but they can see she's got what might have been a "situation" well in hand. The young volunteer is escorted into the building to deliver the papers to the front desk. Dexter remains outside talking into his bull horn at passersby. He winks at the security guard, "This'll get your guys a Pulitzer. Guaranteed. Just remember it's the ol'Dex who brought in the bacon. Do me a favor, honey. Call on your little shoulder phone and tell editorial to send their ace reporter to the FBI offices. We're gonna drop some bomb...s, he catches himself, 'metaphorically'," he corrects himself... "papers, I'm talking papers, M'am, I am. We're going to shame the Feds into doing their job and jail the real crooks. Get off their rusty-dusties. Our little cache makes the Panama Papers look like small potatoes. And, little lady, if I don't get arrested by Elliot Ness and his G-Men, I'm gonna drop off some more copies at the Internal Revenue Service. Then I'm gonna go door to door to all those corporate lobbyists on K Street and let'em know the Dex is puttin' on his hex."

By now, amused, the security guard toys a bit with Dexter, "I'll make sure the big cheeses know you came by, Mr. Boss Man. Stay outta jail."

Dexter charges back onto the bus. He snuggles next to Schotzy. Pookie plays a slow dirge. "We're gonna get GAFA!" Dexter whispers.

End of Chapter 6

John Brown

"No man is free until every man is free." MLK, Jr.

The Hanged Man

Chapter 7
A Most Unhappy Fella

Tuesday, July 28th

Having had to withstand a withering barrage of demands and insults slung by the governor at this meeting of the Louisville Chamber of Commerce, Mayor Craig Trout calmly responds so that everyone in the room can hear. "I do not work for you, in all due respect, Governor. I was voted into office by the good people of Louisville with the backing of local businesses."

"Here, here," several business owners thump the table in front of them or stamp the floor.

"Most of these hardworking owners," continues Craig, "expect to reap the benefits of the visitors who have already begun to flow into town. And, our tax base has grown considerably as several new businesses have sprung up as a result of the Jubilee."

"You need to put country before city," the Governor sputters, "I know on good authority that anarchists are going to disrupt your daily lives."

"Perhaps you can share that intel with our capable law enforcement," Craig nods toward Sheriff Dearborne. They've had weeks to prepare and have informed me they have the situation under control."

The Governor explodes, "You're going to be sorry you didn't listen to me, Trout. Your political career is over."

"So be it," retorts Craig unfazed, "Oh, and by the way, in case you've forgotten, you would only have one vote even if you lived in our city."

"Look, smartass," fumes the Governor, "you're carousing with a bunch of eco-terrorists and commies. Make ya happy?"

At this point the president of the Chamber, Doug Stewart, breaks in to try and bring an end to the increasingly ugly exchange, "The Mayor gets our full support, Governor. We want this next couple of weeks to run smoothly. We flatly reject calling in the National Guard. Not good for business. These are some smart people with a lot to offer us. It's not against the law to come to our town to hold a convention."

From the back of the room Bobby McGrath can't help himself. He hollers, "Exposition. Not convention!"

* *

More and more people gather in the Times Square bleachers to watch the split screens CNN runs in real time tracking the various Critical Mass bikers who are descending on Louisville from all directions. The Olympics are having to play second fiddle. By far the screen garnering the most attention is the one that focuses on the flotilla. CNN has even managed to get a streaming devise on board "*Si Se Puede*". Caroline and DaNeeda welcome the cameraman. They know the value of publicizing the Jubilee. This is a great chance for them to get their message directly to the American people rather than the false narrative that's constantly carried over the airwaves. Besides, they've laughed together, who doesn't like to primp a little bit in front of a camera? All kidding aside, they are aware of the importance of their mission. They've already reached Greenup, Kentucky and are just now passing through the locks. They are happy for a temporary break in the action. After all, the journey so far has been a constant fret for the safety of their charges. "Phew!" exhales Caroline, "We're already in Greenup. I can't believe we've made such good time." She hugs DaNeeda but then stiffens abruptly.

"What, Caroline?" worries DaNeeda, "You seen a ghost?"

"Worse," she points her arm over DaNeeda's shoulder.

DaNeeda turns and looks up at the horizon. She gasps. "Oh my God. A Nor'Easter." The camera pans to the sky in the Northeast. It's ugly, dark and purple. Simultaneously in faraway New York the bleacher crowd gapping at the giant Times Square screen gulps and shutters in unison.

* *

Good to his word Derrick Quince, CEO of Darkwater, personally set out to gather information for the National Security Agency on express orders from General Hikeover, Chief of Staff at the Agency. Proud of the work he does on behalf of his country, Derrick rarely, if ever, questions the legality of some of his missions. The mere fact that deniability has to be built into some of the orders he carries out might give him pause but so far in his career of secret missions he has never said "no" to any assignment. Why would he? He knows in his heart he is a loyal American and patriotic citizen. Those are morals enough. Derrick arrives in Washington D.C. in less than five hours after his meeting with the general. Once here it takes him less than an hour to locate his "target"- the very visible black Cadillac hearse and Dexter's bus. He follows at a safe distance so as not to draw attention to himself. Derrick is already familiar with the area in and around the District of Columbia and Arlington, Virginia. Most of his business has been with the Department Of Defense and contracting privately with weapons manufacturers such as Lockheed/Martin and Northrop Gruman. They have been Darkwater's bread and butter. Of course, the CIA has used his services scores of times but always off the books. Given *carte blanche* by General Hikeover Derrick has already figured out the course of action he will take to quell the treasonous activities of the Dover caravan. He follows them through the city for a couple of hours scoffing at their outrageous attempts to gain publicity. He wonders how they could dare to so openly challenge authority and blatantly try and disrupt law and order. Who are these people? How have they been brought up? If they don't love their country why don't they leave? There was little Derrick could accomplish in broad daylight in a metropolitan area so he decided to gamble. Calculating that the Dover entourage will be taking the shortest route to Louisville once they leave Washington, Derrick consults his map. His Navy Seal tracking instincts tell him they will almost surely be taking Interstate Highway 68. On this impulse Derrick abruptly stops following the caravan and veers his non-descript gray Honda Civic towards the West. Easing through traffic in less than forty-five minutes, deep in thought, he's driving down Highway 68 carefully scouting for a perch where he can get a clear view of the hearse and bus that will soon, by his calculations, be driving by. At a steady pace two hours later he comes to Green Ridge State Forest. "Perfect," he whispers to himself and pulls his car into the first rest stop in order to survey the rolling hills. He gets out of his car and stretches. Right away he notices a service road leading up a steep incline. He inspects closer but determines the road is too rocky to risk getting a flat tire. He looks at his watch. It's a couple of hours before sunset. He goes back to his car. He looks around. He's alone at the rest stop. He opens the trunk to his car and removes a duffle bag which he unzips and takes out his camouflage uniform which he quickly steps into. He zips up the bag and hefts it onto his right shoulder and begins hiking up the path. A hundred or so yards up the hill he spots a group of rocks. He looks back down and has a clear view of Highway 68 about two hundred and fifty maybe three hundred yards away. He ducks behind the rocks and builds a nest where he can wait for his prey. He unzips the duffle and gently, lovingly takes out his trusted bolt action M-24 with an army issued telescopic sight. Derrick has entered into a dream-like mode. His years of training have put his body into an acute awareness of his surroundings. He's on automatic pilot. It's a state of euphoria to which he enters knowing he is carrying out a sacred duty. He caresses the barrel of the rifle and looks down it towards the Highway. Carefully he calibrates the scope to the nth degree. He takes slow, measured breaths. He's unconcerned about the setting sun. He's got night-vision goggles. He's ready. He waits.

* *

Inside the Dover bus Pookie leads the revelers in folk song after folk song. The driver easily keeps pace with the limousine leading the way. Dexter sings loudest and scrubs the washboard he's borrowed from his new tattooed friend. Schotzy requests "Red River Valley". When they come to the line "We will miss your bright eyes and sweet smile..."

Dexter explodes energetically, "That's freedom folks. The song's talkin' about freedom. We can't let it slip away." Next Pookie squeezes out a mournful rendition of "Shenandoah". Dexter croons, "I long to see you...," he's almost crying by the end of the song but barely missing a beat he then belts out a lively "John Brown's Body lies a'mouldering in the grave," and offers anyone who will listen a brief history lesson. "We're not far from Harper's Ferry folks. Ol' J.B. wanted to free all the slaves but they hung'em like a common criminal. If he was still with us today he'd be leadin' the charge to Louisville. We're all slaves to this unforgiving system. Embrace the spirit of John Brown. Embrace freedom." Dexter passes his flask around, "Come on, peeps. This is not a teetotalling caravan." Someone in the middle of the bus who has been enjoying Dexter's antics breaks into "Mine Eyes Have Seen the Glory" and Pookie accompanies. By the chorus the whole bus is chiming in. Just at the peak of "Glory, glory, Hallelujah..." a flurry of loud cracks like a whip snapping. The bus careens violently to the right. Passengers scream. The bus comes to a shrieking halt on the Highway shoulder only yards from a deep ravine.

Derrick methodically picks up his M-24 carbine and hastens to re-holster it. He surveys his little nest to make sure he's leaving no clues. He takes one last glance at the road below. He's pleased with the chaos that has erupted. Mission accomplished. All four of his shots hit their marks. The front and back tires of the hearse are shredded. The limo driver ducks out from behind the steering wheel and scurries to shelter behind a huge rock. The front and back tires of the bus have been blown out. Folks cower below the window line not knowing what to expect. Everyone, that is, except Dexter. He grabs his bull horn and leaps down the steps of the bus. He stands in the middle of the Highway and shouts a challenge that rings out into the evening air, "Come on out, you cowards. I'm here, mano el mano, you chicken shit bastards." Schotzy yells at Dexter begging him to take cover but he's not backing down. Derrick quick hikes to his car and slips away toward Louisville.

End of Chapter 7

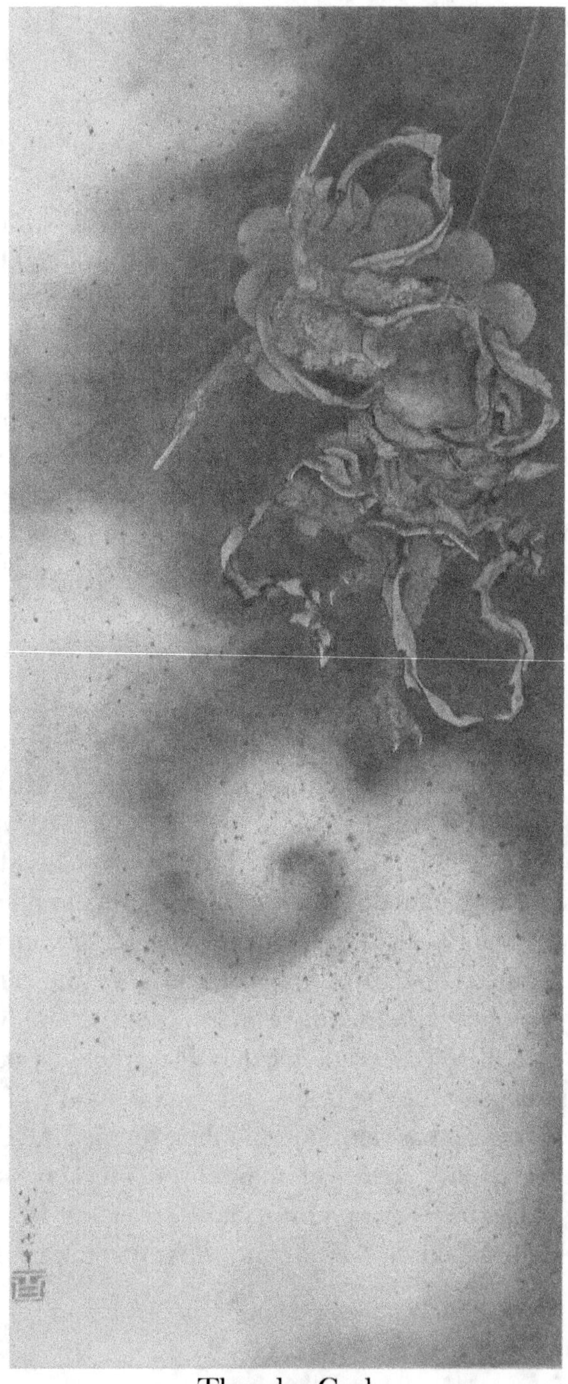

Thunder God

Chapter 8
"It's An Epidemic!"

Wednesday, July 29th

Jubilee fever infects most of the people of Louisville. And, by virtue of the crowds gathering in Times Square the fever is spreading exponentially. There are reports of Critical Mass bike rides in Hungary, France, Germany and Italy. Brazil and Argentina have their own. Hong Kong's Critical Mass circles the city. Cyclists everywhere support the people's demand for an old fashioned Jubilee. In Louisville several new businesses sprout up. For instance, Blue Grass Parking. A local farmer opens up ten acres of fallow land so folks can park their cars and take a shuttle downtown to wherever they are staying. Hotels are solidly booked and the exposition isn't even scheduled to start for another six days. There's been some push back from a few businesses when they were first introduced to the so-called "Jive Five" code-a five dollar cap on certain necessities. This was an idea that Meredith and other Jubilee organizers had come up with to make sure anyone who made the effort to come all the way to Louisville would be able to afford their stay. Some business owners griped that this might impinge on their ability to make a profit. But, when they were shown the numbers they realized that the volume of buyer's they would attract by cooperating with this unwritten agreement would easily make it worth their while. What really clinched the idea was when the musicians and their promoters all agreed not to charge more than five bucks for a concert ticket. Every artist signed the United Nations universal contract that all performers would be paid the same. Foley's Pub set the price of a pint of Guinness at five dollars and all other pints as well. Almost every restaurant in town offers a five-dollar-a-plate special for visitors to fill their bellies.

Mayor Trout speaks enthusiastically at another Chamber meeting, "In all my years in politics I've never seen such heart-warming cooperation.

You guys all deserve a healthy pat on the back. A special thanks to the motel and hotel owners for not gouging. That was a major complaint at the Democratic Convention in Milwaukee a couple weeks ago. I'm not sorry to say, some of those hotels took a bath when boycotts were quickly organized against the gougers. That's the power of social media, need I remind you."

Fred Roth interrupts. Known locally as "The Colonel" because he looks and dresses like the familiar Colonel Sanders from the ads. Not only is he a look-a-like but he owns a couple of chicken franchises. He also owns a costume business with a shop near the University of Kentucky campus. He suggests, "What about a parade? I ain't heard nobody mention nothin' 'bout a parade. Seems only natural, y'all." Several folks nod.

Someone offers, "What about Saturday?" Someone else pipes up, "Yeh. That'd work for me."

"Sure n'uff," encourages the Colonel, "Start at the U.K campus and take it on over to Riverfront Park."

The mayor gets back into the mix, "I defer to Meredith." He hands her the mic.

Checking her phone, she frowns slightly, "We have all sorts of vital workshops on Saturday. I'd sure hate to detract from them."

"What the Sam Hill," the colonel says in character, " We're easy, sleazy, doll face. How'bout Sunday, Honey?"

"Sunday'd be terrific," assures Meredith tactfully ignoring his 1950s retro name calling, "the exhibition will be winding down. We already planned to proclaim that Sunday International Peace Day."

"Well, there you have it, sweet thang, your bowl of cherries with whipped cream on top," the Colonel's pleased, "Let's have us a contest for the most inventive Jubilee costume. We'll need judges. I gladly offer mah services."

"Why you ol' polecat," kids the colonel's longtime friend Sam Watson, "no way you can be judging your own costumes."

"Sam," pouts the colonel, "I'm hurt. I'm genuinely hurt you don't think I can be fair minded."

"Not when there's prize money!" Sam gently but firmly vetoes his friend's judgeship.

* *

A gigantic rescue mission is underway at the Markland locks. A general alarm has blasted over the water ordering all rivercraft ashore until the storm lets up. The water has risen dangerously high in just the past hour. Lightening rips across the sky followed by rolling thunder. This may be familiar to mid-westerners but it sure scares the hell out of DaNeeda and Caroline. They are rapidly becoming aware of the extreme danger flooding can cause. Several of the smaller skiffs have capsized as the current gains speed. Those who have been thrown overboard cling to whatever floats. Caroline and DaNeeda shout directions from the shore but are mostly drowned out by thunderclaps. The rain pours down furiously, in sheets. A family of six barely holds on to the remnants of what was their wooden dream boat. A desperate father begs each of his four children to hold on tightly. His legs kicking like a paddle wheel he steers them towards the shore. His wife loses her grip and gets caught up in the current. Her husband can't see her as her head sinks below the surface. He screams, "She can't swim. Help. She can't swim." Her head bobs up for just an instant. She's choking on water. Again she submerges.

A lock maintenance man working for the Army Corps of Engineers recognizes the danger and in a selfless instant dives into the river and pulls the gagging woman to the surface. The father pushes the children to the edge of the lock where several workers lift them to safety. A cheer goes up as their fellow worker brings the wife to the shore. She's hauled in like a big tuna but overjoyed to rejoin her family.

Caroline cries with relief, "This could have ended the whole enterprise."

DaNeeda shutters, "All life rests on such a thin layer of ice."

This comment must have come from her unconscious and Caroline immediately picks up on it. "Well, you can blame I.C.E. for forcing our people into these circumstances." She's referring of course to Immigration and Customs Enforcement. "I hope they melt."

End of Chapter 8

Southern Comfort Tent City

Chapter 9
Southern Hospitality, AKA Tent City

Thursday, July 30th

Derrick Quince puts his Navy Seal training into practice. He knows how to blend in with a crowd and not draw attention. Likewise, when tracking someone he knows how to stay at a safe distance. He drives a decade old Gray Honda Civic. Nothing fancy. Last night, because all the hotels were filled to capacity, he was forced to sleep in the front of his beater with the seat reclined. This morning he stops at a filling station to freshen up. Looking into a restroom mirror he decides not to shave his stubble. Could help him blend with the scraggily crowd he might be mingling with. He downs an energy bar and gets behind the wheel. He drives back towards downtown. Today might be his time to infiltrate. Find the leaders the general is so keen to study. Derrick thinks back to what the general said about his father. What did happen in the Vietnam jungle when his father was captured? Whatever it was, it contributed to his remoteness. He'd always been a disciplinarian, even before he went to Nam, but when he came back he could be harsh, extremely harsh, bordering on the cruel, to whoever wouldn't toe his line. Derrick snaps out of his daydream when he notices a group of college-age students exit from a coffee shop near the UK campus. His instincts tell him to follow their SUV. Staying several car lengths behind, even allowing some cars to get between his Honda and the SUV, he tracks them. They lead him down Main St. and turn left on Muhammed Ali Blvd. Within minutes they arrive at "The Gardens". Derrick trails off and finds a shady spot in a distant part of the parking lot. He grabs his thermos and takes a slug of hot coffee. Then, he reaches into the glove compartment and takes out his binoculars. He stares at the front entrance. He confirms to himself,

"This is the beehive!" After several minutes Meredith steps out. Derrick's jaw drops. "Bingo!" he exhales, "The Queen Bee!" He recognizes her immediately. They have a history of nasty confrontations. She led the demonstrations against his training facility that he planned to open in Southern California. She caused long delays and finally the complete closing down of what was supposed to be a lucrative project. She's cost him money. Lots of it. His warrior instincts tell him he's owed a little payback. On second thought-a lot of payback.

* *

Bobby McGrath supervises a crew of at least twenty as they strategically position port-o-potties along the fairways of the Southern Comfort Country Club. "Let's get the yellow tape around the greens, boys and girls," he urges, "They must be clearly marked." Bobby squats down near a sand trap. He pulls gently at a clump of saw grass. He frowns, clearly disturbed, "Damn, why do they spread all this chemical crap on what should be a naturally beautiful sheen of Kentucky Bluegrass?" Dismayed, he shakes his head. Bobby's scheduled to lead the pesticide teach-in on Monsanto and their life-destroying RoundUp-a particular bad actor. McGrath has invited the head Country Club groundskeeper and his crew. He hopes he'll be able to convincingly convey the message to them of how environmentally destructive are these chemicals currently being used. He goes back to instructing his lads and lasses who are all eager apprentice naturalists. Their task today is to make habitable the first-ever Jubilee Tent City.

* *

Meredith drives her hybrid Toyota Camry to Foley's Pub. She's jonesing for some early morning bangers and mash. Derrick follows and discreetly parks a half block away where he can monitor who comes and goes through the swinging doors that have been a trademark of the Pub since its opening. Derrick takes careful notes and records his observations which he will shortly pass on to the general who he is sure waits anxiously at the New York NSA headquarters. Derrick has already identified who he knows to be one of the principal leaders which makes her his necessary target. He knows what he, Derrick Quince, super patriot, lover of God, Country, and family, will do to fulfill his destiny. And, the destiny of the nation he loves and serves.

* *

Inside Foley's Pub it's like a super bowl frenzy. Already, the suds are flowing from the taps. The $5 pints are more popular than Carter's little liver pills and probably more effective particularly when coupled with a home state Kentucky Bourbon boilermaker. Foley's owner Art, son of the founder Malachy Foley, has even brewed a special batch of craft beer and labeled it Jubilee Ale. Pookie fingers her squeeze box. She's joined by a local fiddler and bass player. Some Irish step dancers are warming up on the tiny stage in the back room. Schotzy's comfortable in a nearby booth nursing a pint of Jubilee Ale. Dexter's throwing darts with some locals. Several city officials are taking part in the festivities, obviously enjoying themselves. A loud cheer reverberates throughout the pub. Marly shouts out gleefully, "They've made it! They're through customs. Seven of'em." A roar of approval bounces off the pub walls. Marly's referring to the Russian radical feminist band "Pussy Riot". After six months of tense negotiations they've been given visas to tour America in a series of concerts. Their very first gig will be right here in Louisville only two days from now on Saturday afternoon in the sold-out coliseum. They're sharing top billing with who else? The regrouped Dixie Chicks.

* *

An even louder cheer erupts from the stands in New York City's Times Square. CNN's covering live from JFK airport. Pussy Riot comes out waving victoriously to their thousands of fans who clog the entrance. The Dixie Chicks are there high-fiving and hugging. Sisters in music and sisters in resistance.

* *

A local band from Henry Clay High School plays *De Colores* on the southern bank of the Ohio. They are there to greet the weary flotilla. The dinghy people disembark at the Louisville Wheel after their historic journey. Earlier in the week Mayor Trout declared Louisville to be a sanctuary city. The governor was furious and vowed to rescind the order. It was sure to be a state constitutional battle. Craig knows that Sheriff Dearborne and his men will honor the sanctuary rules. It's not their job to meddle with anyone's immigration status. Craig stands just below the towering wheel shaking hands and hugging tired river refugees. Four local churches have set up a soup kitchen to serve hot food to hungry travelers. Overwhelmed with emotion Caroline and DaNeeda cry quietly, "You see," chokes DaNeeda, "I told you, Americans are good people."

* *

Derrick Quince frowns and grinds his teeth while watching scads of people coming and going through the front entrance of Foley's. He takes his encrypted phone from his breast pocket and calls General Hikeover, "I can isolate a target."

Hikeover whispers, "You have to make your move before Saturday. We can't let them have the concert."

"I can stop it," Derrick confidently tells the general.

"This is code red," the general's eyes dart, "you are delegated to do what needs to be done. God be with you."

"Roger," confirms the former Navy Seal, "over and out." Derrick Quince, CEO of Darkwater, starts his car and deliberately drives through the city and to the outskirts carefully searching for a remote area far away from the possibility of any surveillance cameras.

End of Chapter 9

Sacrifice of Isaac

Night Prayers in Mecca

Chapter 10
"Beyond the Pale"

Friday, July 31st.

One hundred? Two hundred? Maybe as many as three hundred yellow cabs descend on Time Square from all different directions. They are here to celebrate Eid al-Adha, the Muslim holiday taking place during the Hajj-the annual pilgrimage to Mecca. The cab drivers halt their cabs wherever they are precisely at high noon. They get out and kneel down facing East in the direction of Mecca. Their prayers last less than two minutes after which they get back in their cabs and disperse. The bleacher crowd is momentarily distracted from the giant screen and gets a live action Broadway show. The real drama though is off-Broadway. The Muslim Holiday commemorates the willingness of Abraham to sacrifice his son Isaac or was it Ismael? The debate continues but the crux of the argument should not be who but rather why? God's command? Says who? This has been a philosophical debate for time immemorial in Islam, Judaism and Christianity. Was this an order given by a God gone mad or a hallucination by Abraham who had lost his cookies? Was he hearing voices or what? At any rate, debating the story someone would inevitably ask, "Doesn't Isaac have a say so in his own sacrifice? If you feel so compelled to follow an order to sacrifice something how about you cut off your own arm, Abe, if it's obedience you want to prove. Why use someone else? And, it begs the question. Are orders to be followed unquestionably? Blind faith in authority? Obedience at all costs? Who's authority? Doesn't every person have to answer for his or her individual action? This conundrum was raised over and over at the Nuremberg Nazi war trials. "I was just following orders," was not, is not and never will be a valid reason for carrying out an inhumane act. During the Vietnam War fragging became a powerful deterrent to any officer issuing an unethical order. The word "fragging" comes from a grenade fragment which enlisted men began tossing into an officer's tent if he issued an immoral or even a just plain stupid order. And, finally, not to forget Abraham, why would he or why should he follow an order from anyone who refused to clearly identify Himself, Herself, or Itself?

* *

"Why'd he change his name?" Dex asks Schotzy as he leads her through the front entrance of the Muhammad Ali Museum. The modern steel and glass building glistens in the noonday sun.

"It was the military build-up for the Vietnam War. Young men were being drafted to fight a war against Asians thousands of miles away. They'd never heard of the place and were being given conflicting reasons for what this war was all about," Schotzy patiently explains.

"Hey," Dex shows he's thought a lot about this himself. He quotes facetiously from the Rudyard Kipling poem, "Theirs is not to question why, theirs is but to do and die!"

"You got it, Dex," Schotzy affirms. "There's always someone willing to send someone else into battle while preserving their own skin in a high command post."

"So," continues Dexter, "young Cassius Clay had a functional brain on top of his shoulders. He wasn't about to follow some unhinged order."

"He reasoned like this," enthuses Schotzy, "'Why should I, a young Black man, travel thousands of miles away to shoot at a yellow man for some crinkly old white man?' Particularly when he could see Black men in his own city of Louisville were being oppressed and killed by the white man."

Dex intervenes, "So he converted to Islam and changed his name from Cassius Clay..."

"Sure did," confirms Schotzy, "at the height of his profession. He was at the time undisputed heavyweight champion of the world."

"Whoa, that took some balls," admires Dex.

"Sure did," agrees Schotzy. "Uncle Sam didn't know what to do."

"Spit in his shoe," says Dex flippantly.

The odd couple spends the next couple of hours walking through the various museum exhibits with Dexter detailing to Schotzy certain points of interest.

Late in the afternoon Schotzy muses, "You know Dex, another Clay represented Kentucky in the Senate. Henry Clay."

"Who's he?" Dex is sure Schotzy's getting ready to tell him something interesting about history.

"He was a smooth-tongued politician..."

"Aren't they all," interjects Dex.

Schotzy continues, "The Kentucky contradiction in full array. Henry was a virulent racist, particularly against the Native American population. Ironic isn't it? They shared the same surname but one spewed hate and the other an outspoken internationalist with a heart of gold." Schotzy shakes her head.

"Float like a butterfly, sting like a bee," Dex locks arms with Schotzy, "Come on Mama, let's invade Foley's."

"I'm ready, little man, but, please," she cautions, "pace yourself, Dexter, pace yourself."

* *

Hundreds of tents line the fairways of the Southern Comfort Country Club. Port-o-potties are placed in roughs at intervals all around the golf course. Bobby Mcgrath walks out of the clubhouse shoulder to shoulder with Sam Carpenter.

"I know you love your club, Sam, but some of these pesticides are bound to seep into your groundwater. It can't be avoided. Maybe not today but years down the line. The next generation's going to pay, and pay dearly." Bobby keeps up a rapid pace as he has lots of inspections he still has to conduct.

Carp pants trying to keep pace, "We've been discussing just this issue at our last couple of board meetings. I'm glad you've convinced our crew to attend the Monsanto workshop."

McGrath stops for a moment to let Carp catch up, "We've got a lot to unlearn and then learn again. If we learn nothing else, we need to learn and teach the importance of protecting our fresh water."

* *

Derrick Quince finds an isolated spot on the Eastern bank of the Ohio just South of the Crescent Hill Treatment Plant. From his vantage point he can see the Louisville water tower.

"Mi Wiconi," he spits out derisively. "What did the Indians know that Western science couldn't figure out? The river is the source of drinking water for 3 million people. A lot more than 'they' serviced." Quince continues to vent out loud for several more seconds then, to calm his inner anger, he sits down in a full lotus position and takes deep breaths. He can't calm his turbulent mind, "Why are these anarchists coming to Louisville? What can they hope to accomplish? If they just followed the rules." He cascades from thought to thought. "Hikeover's a clown. Yeh, my father was a great man. Unlike you, General, he commanded the respect of his men. He knew the value of discipline. Cross him and you paid a price. He'd sacrifice you quicker than a jackrabbit." As the sunsets behind the rolling hills Derrick exclaims out loud,   "These lost souls are under the influence of the Anti-Christ!"

* *

Pre-dawn in Mecca, Saudi Arabia. The call to prayer over the loudspeakers reverberates across the city. Millions of visitors in this Holy setting kneel in prayer.

Tens of thousands of visitors to New York cram Times Square and stare gobsmacked at the big screen witnessing this incredible dedication to a Supreme being. The planet yawns and exudes a cathartic Ohmmmmm!

* *

If human energy could levitate a building, Foley's Pub would be ten feet off the ground. TV screens behind the bar are tracking as many of the Critical Mass bikers as they are able. It's like the Tour De France but spread out in many different directions. Just a few days ago the Pride ride had left Sheridan Square, West Village, New York, home of the Stonewall tavern where the 1969 riot broke out. The Pride breaks the tape in Louisville. They outpaced the Puerto Rican Mass that was slowed by an enormous influx of riders along the way. Many also joined the Pride pack but they were able to nimbly keep pace. Artie, owner of Foley's, has put up a large board in the backroom next to the dart board. He's been handicapping each Mass and posts the odds on a regular basis. Pride came in as a 2-1 favorite. Right now smart money's riding on the Elvis brigade. They have been gaining speed since the Nashville pit stop.

On a small stage also in the backroom comedian Dale Bumpers closes out an early set, "Y'all know that group that calls themselves M.A.D., Mothers Against Drunks, I've joined another group, more to my liking. It's called D.A.M. Drunks Against Mothers!" There are a few groans and chortles. Someone yells, "Bottoms Up, Mother Fucker," which gets more laughs than Dale was able to garner. He takes it in good humor, "Y'all come back for the next set and I'll tell you what happens when Jesus and Mohammad enter a bar."

"Tell us now," a lady from shouts from the booth next to Schotzy and Pookie.

"No can do," insists Bumpers. "My jokes are proprietary and can only be told during an official set. This one's over. See you in an hour."

Pookie's dressed from head to toe in Emerald green. She's next up to perform. Before she goes on stage Schotzy wonders, "Have you seen Dex?"

"He was tossing down pints not too long ago," offers Pookie.

Schotzy grimaces, "This early? I told him to pace himself."

"In this environment," Pookie shakes her head, "Come on, Schotzy."

Just then Dexter emerges from the men's room in the hallway. Pookie laughs hysterically, "You gotta be kidding."

Schotzy, anxious, "What? Whad'ya see?"

"Dexter has returned. You should see him," Pookie chuckles.

"Tell me," Schotzy's clearly frustrated.

"He's all decked out in an outrageous Leprechaun outfit. Wherever in the world did he find it? Complete with corncob pipe." Pookie tries her best to do justice to Dexter's costume so Schotzy can enjoy the spectacle.

Dexter command's the room's attention. With his arms he silently gestures for bodies to separate and clear a path for him.

"Drum roll," he shouts. He takes a deep breath, puts his head down and does a double cartwheel neatly sticking it at Pookie's and Schotzy's booth. He's greeted with hoots, hollers and applause. "Erin Go Bragh!" Dexter's in his element and definitely in his cups.

Schotzy sighs, "Pace yourself, Dex. Pace yourself."

"Too late, Mama. It wasn't a pot'a'gold at the end of that rainbow but a bucketful of mushrooms," confesses Dex beginning to drool.

"Oh, Dexter, you didn't. Not again." Schotzy reaches out and tightly grasps his hand.

"Oh, yes, Mama, I did."

* *

You would be forgiven if you thought burning a cross in a country field was a thing of the past. But, on the outskirts of small town in Southern Ohio not far from the River a gathering of Klan members solemnly repeats an oath to the preservation of the white race-whatever that means. One could also be forgiven for thinking this is some kind of joke. Who would take seriously someone dressed in a white sheet and wearing a pointed hat like a cliché schoolroom dunce? But this is the 21st century and mankind seems to be rapidly de-civilizing. Hate is served as a breakfast cereal with no sugar coating. Torturers are elevated to key positions in the military and intelligence communities. Lots of good minds lament the human condition but no one knows for sure how we got here. Was it over-exposure to violent video games that show a remarkable lack of reverence for human life. But, there's no direct correlation. Lots of countries have violent video games but they do not host regular random shootings. Maybe it's the rampant supply Big Pharma drugs to which people get addicted to mask the pain of existence-uppers, downers, anti-depressants-whatever. Some correlation but definitely not a direct link. What drives a person to purchase a gun and shoot people at random? Who can hate that much?"

* *

"Mudpeople continue to pollute our gene pool," angrily shouts a male voice behind a mask that looks much more ridiculous than scary. He continues to regurgitate this gibberish in a monotone for several minutes. He's addressing a small but virulent group of racists who are gathered for the express purpose of drawing up a plan to disrupt the Jubilee that everyone is talking about. As he rattles on, he exposes his ignorance of the fact that intermarriages amongst tribes and races has strengthened rather than weakened the gene pool. Hemophilia caused by royal family incest is a clear example. Case closed."

* *

"Told you," says Sheriff Dearborne in response to Meredith's surprise to see him in Foley's this Friday evening. "My days off are Saturday and Sunday." He clinks glasses with Marly, Meredith and Bobby McGrath in a booth toward the front of the bar.
"You are full of surprises," Meredith returns his engaging smile. "Somehow I pictured a teetotaler."

"Must be the badge, but I assure you I don't drink on duty," Ted motions to the waitress to bring the table another round.

"Spoke like an eagle scout," kids Meredith.

"Slainte'," toasts McGrath and drains his glass.

Dexter stumbles past the table. "You know'em?" The Sheriff's concerned.

"Not really," Meredith strokes her chin, "he showed up with that spiffy black hearse that carried the Dover papers." She takes a deep swig of her beer.

"I read about them," says Ted, "An expose was published in this morning's Courier-Dispatch."

Meredith likes that the Sheriff seems to be up on current political news. Not all cops are. She probes further. "So, do you have a family, Ted?"

Sheriff Ted looks at Marly and says affably, "I was jilted at the altar."

Marly laughs, "A bit dramatic aren't we, Theodore?"

"I'm a bachelor. To answer your question," Ted says frankly.

"Well, Queen Mab, there's your opening," jibes McGrath.

Meredith blushes ever so slightly," I was just making small talk."

"Way out of character for you," McGrath continues to dig, "Your turn."

Meredith glares at McGrath. She's not comfortable in the emotional spotlight and not used to it.

Bobby continues to goad her, "Come on, tell us about your love life."

Ted's ears perk.

"That's enough, Bobby," flustered Meredith's relieved that the waitress has arrived with the refills. She catches a sidelong glance at Ted.

In the backroom Pookie stokes the revelers,

"Camptown ladies sing this song,

Doo-dah, Doo-dah,

Camptown racetrack five miles long,

Oh doo-dah day.

I come down here with my hat caved in,

Doo-dah,

Go back home with my pocket full of tin.

Oh, Doo-dah Day.

Gwine to run all night,

Gwine to run all day,

I bet my money on a bob-tail nag,

Somebody bet on the Bay."

Ted listens to the song booming from the back- room, "That's almost our theme song here in Louisville. Too bad Mr. Foster had some antiquated racist ideas. He sure had a knack for songwriting."

Meredith likes the way he speaks frankly without beating around the bush. He turns to her, "If you can find the time, maybe you'd like to drive down to Stephen's old Kentucky home. It's a museum only about 45 minutes south of here."

"I'd like that," says Meredith without a moment's hesitation. Marly and McGrath exchange knowing looks.

I'm off tomorrow and Sunday," repeats Dearborne.

"Sunday's a date," confirms Meredith.

"9am too early?" poses Ted.

"Works for me." Meredith closes the deal.

End of Chapter 10

Greed

Chapter 11
Cuffed and Cornered

Saturday, August 1st, shortly past Midnight

Louisville, Kentucky.

Maybe time to take a deep breath. Let's not gloss over the fact that July is named after Julius Caesar, the Roman power-hungry would-be dictator who was famously assassinated by a group of men who thought they were protecting democracy. And, August is named after his adopted son and Emperor Augustus who reigned in the years prior to the Roman Empire's descent into hell and eventual downfall. There were several emperors (Nero and Caligula come to mind)who partook in outrageous sexual exploitation of their subjects. And there was rampant corruption. Can we not draw an easy comparison with the United States? Never has there been such manipulation of an economy as the Oligarchs practice in this country where the catchphrase "Greed is Good" actually caught on. The 2008 financial meltdown exposed this fraud and yet the banksters were allowed to dip into the public trough and give themselves million dollar bonuses rewarding instead of punishing their blatant financial skullduggery. And, the sexual "peccadillos" (hardly the right word when talking human trafficking of boys and girls in their early teens)! Everybody's heard the old saw that "history repeats itself". Are we there yet? Has the U.S. government gone too far in their aggressive militarism, and their involvement in propping up a thoroughly corrupt and disgusting system? You be the judge this early August morning around 1AM.

Dexter's mind spins like a top as he trippingly stumbles out the back entrance of Foley's Pub. The parking lot's jammed with cars. He staggers, bouncing off fender after fender setting off a cascade of car alarms. His stomach rumbles. He gags. He can't hold back an eruption. Chunks of fluid flow from his pie hole and splash on the concrete. He falls face down into his own puke. Barely conscious, lying prostate, dizzy he peers beneath the car next to where he has fallen. He struggles to focus. Wide-eyed, "WETIKO!!!" His shout booms through the back alleys of downtown Louisville. A rookie cop assigned to patrol Foley's rushes into the back parking lot. Gun drawn, he confronts a shaken Dexter lying in his own vomit. He mumbles repeatedly, "Under the car, under the car..." and manages to point. The young officer kneels at the front of the car and peers underneath. He levels his gun and orders, "Out, get out. You are covered. Show your hands." Scared and still crouching the young cop speaks into his shoulder mic, "Back up, now. Foley's Pub parking lot, hurry."

* *

Inside Foley's Sheriff Ted's phone vibrates. He apologizes to his friends in the booth, "Sorry, on call," and checks his phone. His head jerks towards the back room. Without a word of explanation he vaults from his seat, squirms through the crowd and charges out the back exit. A small crowd of onlookers has already gathered. Officer Gary Galenski shouts an order to the man from underneath the car who is now standing spreckled in Dexter's puke, "Keep your hands in the air."

Sheriff Ted arrives with his gun drawn, "Gary, Gary..."

The young rookie's relieved to hear a familiar voice, "I'm so glad to see you, sir. I wasn't sure what to do next."

Both officers keep their pistols trained on the masked man dressed in an all-black spandex body suit.

"Keep'em in the air," commands Ted. "You did good, Gary. Keep your gun on him." Dearborne holsters his pistol and moves in on the culprit who he grabs and cuffs in a couple of swift moves.

Lots of curious spectators are by now mulling about wondering about the commotion. One or two car alarms are still annoyingly blaring. Meredith, Marly and McGrath followed the Sheriff and are standing by. Meredith says to Marly, "That's my car!"

Once Ted gets the wannabe Ninja warrior cuffed he instructs Officer Galinsky to search around and under the car. Gary squats down with his flash-light. He points first at Dexter who's snoring rather loudly. Then, almost gagging, he peers under the Toyota Prius. He gasps, "Sir, we better move everybody back. Now! There's a bomb underneath that's looks powerful enough to blow the shit out of all of us."

Ted's voice booms, "Everybody stand back. Clear the parking lot. Now." There's some pushing and shoving and back peddling but the parking lot clears with no panic.

"Great work, Gary," Ted takes over, "We'll get the bomb squad here. I'd like you to tape off the whole area. He squares his captive and tears off the face mask. He gapes, "Derrick Quince!"

Standing far back but still able to see, Meredith freezes, then blurts out, "Derrick Quince!"

* *

Around the world crowds are gathering on the 1st of August by the Roman calendar. The moon, waxing gibbous, as the globe turns. Cities stir. Herds of people gather in town squares everywhere on the planet. It's like a volcano beginning to rumble. The human spirit of survival is desperately trying to break out of its cocoon. It has eaten everything in sight but finally wrapped itself in silk. The human butterfly is ready to emerge. It will have to struggle mightily to flutter its wings. The calm, peaceful, spiritual tsunami will demand everyone's attention.

* *

At the New York National Security headquarters General Hikeover has just been informed by Todd Marcher that their asset Derrick Quince has been taken into police custody.

Hikeover reacts, "We've got to lawyer him up, now. Keep my fingerprints off."

"Yes, sir," snaps Marcher wondering if he, himself, might get caught up in a blame game.

"Take this," Hikeover hands Todd a slip of paper. It's a direct number to DOD legal. Don't mention my name."

He turns to Jacob, "Get me the commander of the helicopter crew at Fort Knox."

* *

A Ku Klux Klan rally fizzles in Buck-Eye Park in the city of Portsmouth, Ohio. There are many more protesting Shawnee State college students than there are Klansmen. Hate is tucked under the covers, swept under the carpet, so to speak. There's a peaceful moment on this minute portion of the planet, at least for now.

* *

Times Square's not even waiting for New Year's Eve. Tourists join native New Yorkers to clog the streets. The bleachers are choc-a-block. Folks watch Critical Mass Bikers close in on Louisville. They cheer for their favorite. They eagerly await for the upbeat music of Pussy Riot and the Dixie Chicks which is scheduled to get underway in less than four hours.

* *

"What you are asking me to do, Meredith, is flatly impossible," Ted shakes his head.

"Ted, this is so very important. I need to talk with him one on one. Far away from prying ears. It's vital," beseeches Meredith.

"He's already lawyered up. Besides which it's too risky. Not to mention beyond all protocol," protests the sheriff.

"Ted, let his lawyer know I'll consider dropping all charges if I can get just a few hours with him alone," implores Meredith.

Ted holds up his hands as if to stop her, "Hey, you might drop charges but the City never will. Don't forget we found that rifle in his trunk. Most likely the same gun used to terrorize the Dover caravan."

"But, ...," Meredith tries to break in.

"And that bomb, big enough to take out ten, fifteen cars. You'd be a fried pretzel, Meredith. He's a fraternal brother. A Navy Seal. We trained together. He took the same oath that I took. We swore to uphold the constitution of the United States."

Meredith stops the sheriff with a hard squeeze of his arm. "I can tell you are disillusioned and disgusted by the behavior of your brother in arms. I have a good feeling about you. You're honest. So, let me explain why I think it's vitally important that I meet with him. My parents were lifelong political activists. They lived during the time our government executed Julius and Ethel Rosenberg..."

"I've studied that case," Ted interjects.

"They had opposed the dropping of the Atom bombs on Hiroshima and Nagasaki. They feared the annihilation of our species."

Ted nods listening intently.

"My parents knew what Ethel and Julius were trying to do. Went to meetings with them. After the Rosenbergs were arrested my parents networked with shamans of various cultures trying to tamp down the cold war which was always threatening to turn hot with the press of a finger. They opposed the Korean War-worried about a clash of titans-China and the USA. Then I came along, Ted. Three months premature. My parents detected something unusual about me. They shared their observations with the elders of the Shinnecock Tribe of Native Americans on the Eastern tip of Long Island. I was declared a savant. And, when I was only five years old shamans from many different tribes and cultures came to declare the coming of universal world peace. They built a huge bonfire. I sat cross-legged in front of the fire as close as I could get without getting burned. The heat was intense. I talked in tongues, saying things I could never have heard in my few short years. Black Elk spoke through me. Everyone concurred. The voice was genuine."

Ted is clueless on how to respond. Meredith recognizes his puzzled look. "Can you understand? We are at another crossroads in civilization. The haters have to let go and the lovers have to forgive-not forget-but forgive..."

"Otherwise...," Ted says finishing her thought, "humans will never get out of the cycle of violence."

"Yes," replies Meredith triumphantly, "you get it. We have to convince Derrick Quince to get it, too. He's a leader. We need him."

Ted assures Meredith, "I'll talk with his lawyer."

* *

Ft. Knox, Kentucky. Captain LaShandra Washington faces General Hikeover on a large screen monitor. Captain Washington commands a helicopter crew out of the Air Force base in Ft. Knox.

Hikeover urgently addresses her, "You need to understand the importance of this mission, Captain. You are the last domino against chaos and anarchy. This concert cannot take place." Hikeover impatiently waits for a response.

LaShandra hesitates not certain that the general has finished speaking. Finally she says, "Are you giving me a direct order, Sir?"

"Yes, I'm giving you a direct order." The general's clearly annoyed.

"Well, Sir, you need to be a little bit more specific," LaShandra continues cautiously.

The general cajoles, "The spray has been tested numerous times. It's non-lethal. Hardly any side-effects."

"I think, Sir, the order needs to go through central command." She voices her misgivings.

"There is no time for that, Captain Washington. This is a matter of National Security." The general's adamant.

"I will clear it with my superior officer when he gets here, Sir." LaShandra wants to end the encounter.

"You will not check with anybody else. Whoever you think you need to talk to, I am their superior officer. Nobody can countermand my order. Get airborne! That is an order!" The general turns beet red before the screen goes black.

* *

This Saturday in Louisville's like a carnival. The exhibition will kick off in just a few days. Lots of eager anticipation for the concert later in the day but right now most of the focus is on all the colorful critical mass bike riders that have arrived. They've all agreed to circle several times around Louisville displaying their individual banners and placards. Obviously rehearsed, the one hundred Elvises from that brigade sing song after song of the King's-<u>Heartbreak Hotel</u>, <u>Blue Suede Shoes</u>, <u>Don't Be Cruel</u> and <u>All Shook Up</u>. The pride Critical Mass carries a huge rainbow banner and a first place placard.

* *

Three helicopters are perched on the runway of the Ft. Knox Air Force tarmac. A ground crew attaches a huge cannister to the underbelly of each chopper. Second in command and LaShandra's co-pilot, Lt. Danny Savoy, turns to her and quips, "I heard the boys refer to the liquid as "Boob Beverage."

"Boob Beverage, what in the fuck does that mean, Danny?"

"My reaction, exactly," says Danny, "so I asked around. This shit is supposed to render people stupid and temporarily immobile."

"Like the boob tube, I get it," says LaShandra in disbelief, "we're supposed to swoop down and spray the whole soccer stadium! Wow, I don't know, Danny." The blades of the choppers begin to churn.

* *

Followed by several camera crews and scores of fans The Dixie Chicks mingle with migrant workers and flotilla survivors. A temporary shelter has been set up in Franklin Park. Since Mayor Trout declared Louisville a sanctuary city no one has to fear a raid from ICE. Caroline, DaNeeda and the rest of the fearless flotilla contingent will be unhindered to plead their case at the Jubilee exhibition. But first, they'll hear resistance music at the concert in just over an hour. All flotilla folks have been given free tickets.

* *

Airborne the choppers head north towards Louisville, locked and loaded. LaShandra's having difficulty processing General Hikeover's order. She's been left no wiggle room. In her mind she pores over her responsibility. She's served twice in Iraq and hated every minute. But, she's a soldier. She follows orders. Is this any different she wonders over and over. The three choppers close in on Louisville. Lt. Savoy navigates. The noise of the rotor blades confines them to mostly shouting and pointing. Danny waves to get LaShandra's attention. He points and shouts, "Ali Museum, Ali Museum."

LaShandra peers down. The sun glistens off the museum roof. It's a gut check for LaShandra. All her life she's had one hero whom she's idolized-Muhammed Ali, The Greatest. In school she'd written many papers about his life and his tribulations. She's memorized his six principles: confidence, dedication, conviction, giving, respect and spirituality. Where was the honor in gassing her own people? Non-lethal! What a load of bull shit. She channels the Champ, "Why would a Black woman, listen to a grumpy old white man who doesn't know shit about the struggle for equality?" LaShandra looks at Danny and gives the thumbs down signal. She abruptly turns her chopper around and heads back towards Ft. Knox. The other two choppers follow her. Danny's astonished look requires some explanation. LaShandra shakes her head and shouts at the top of her lungs, "I ain't doin' it!"

End of Chapter 11.

Ghost

Devil Pater

Chapter 12
Armageddon Avoided by Consensus

Sunday, August 2

General Hikeover is abruptly removed from his command post in New York City. For all their faults and horrendous unforgivable mistakes in instigating and perpetuating avoidable war after avoidable war for the past half century the military still sometimes come out on the right side of history. Maybe it's the law of averages. They make decisions by consensus. They call themselves the Joint Chiefs of Staff. No one person at the top of a pyramid but several heads of departments coming together to make what will hopefully be the right decision on behalf of the people they are supposed to be serving. So, when it was revealed that General Hikeover had been acting unilaterally he was immediately stripped of his command and court martial proceedings begun. He had clearly crossed a line in ordering "Boob Juice" sprayed on citizens who were peacefully assembling. And, when it was further revealed that he was the quote "brains" unquote, behind the incredibly stupid plot to bomb a civilian establishment with intent to kill he was tossed into the brig to await trial. To make some amends the joint chiefs agreed that the entire Department of Defense, all divisions, would aid and abet the Jubilee. After all, it was obvious, this is an event that the American people, the entire world, for that matter, devoutly wish to happen. A democratic consensus? So be it declared the brass.

* *

"That was a great concert," rasps a subdued Dexter nursing yet another hangover with an icepack on top of his skull.

"How would you know?" chides Schotzy in good humor, "You slept through most of it."

"I did?" asks Dex genuinely unaware. He turns to Pookie who sits by the 12th floor window of their large suite that they booked months in advance. "Pook-a-Dook, can you hum a gentle version of a Pussy Riot tune? Keep it real slow and real low."

Pookie picks up her accordion and sets it in her lap. "No such animal. Those gals is wild childs!"

"Something sweet, Snooks, gentle, puhlease." Dex lies back on the sofa.

Schotzy suggests, "How 'bout 'My Old Kentucky Home' but drop the darkie reference iffen ya don't mind."

Pookie hums, "Way down upon the Suwanee River...,"

Schotzy reminds her pals, "Another concert tonight."

Dexter moans.

* *

Dusk on a hill in Louisville's back country. Derrick Quince sits on a log and looks sullenly out over the valley below. Meredith gathers firewood, lots of it, for a commanding bond fire she'll ignite shortly. She calls back to Quince, "Ted insisted you have on the ankle bracelet. Sorry 'bout that, Rick," Meredith uses his nickname, purposefully. She knows they are about to engage in a battle of attrition. Two souls who view the world differently. She makes the first move on the chess board obviously trying to soften him up. Derrick, a seasoned veteran of many battles, does not take the bait. He maintains a stone face. He doesn't even acknowledge that he's heard her.

Meredith tries another gambit, "Let me cut to the chase, Derrick. She sits beside him on the log. "You are a proven leader of men. The sheriff's told me of your exploits as a Seal." Derrick stares at her coldly.

"He was flat against my meeting with you. I begged him. Pleaded. Wanna know why?" Quince maintains an icy stare.

"If you and I can come to some sort of mutual agreement-a compromise on our values, principles-our outlook on how the world should play out-I honestly feel there is hope for humanity." She pauses. "I know, it sounds dramatic. But if we <u>can't</u> come to terms and we humans continue to damage the planet we are doomed as a species." As the sun sets in the West Meredith reaches forward with her lighter and flicks. The kindling begins to crackle and moments later the flames lick upward.

The fire blazes. Meredith tacks, "There are at least two sides to every issue. Agreed?" Derrick shows no signs of responding. "Hot-cold, high-low, summer-winter, war-peace,...hate-love."

Quince is still stone silent. Meredith improvises. "What is America if not a dream? We are a beautiful mix of cultures, all dreamers. I requested this meeting because, like I said, you are a leader, and I don't have to tell you, humanity needs leaders to steer us in a healthy direction. Not into war and reigns of terror. You know there are sixty million refugees on this planet as we sit here. Driven from their homes by bombing, terrorism by so many different means. It has to stop, Derrick. You can help stop this. You have that kind of power."

Quince turns from the flames and stares at Meredith. Their two sets of eyes sparkle in the reflection of the flames.

"Yes, power, Mr. Quince. I thought that might tickle your brain. It's about power, isn't it? Not about the Benjamins but about power. Oh, the Benjamins to be sure, they are important because they symbolize power. But you've had your fill and you know, in the end money is a weak symbol of power, isn't it, Derrick? It doesn't do shit but build up a fake front. A false image. Real power is deep within not out on the surface."

He tries to stare through her. Does he hate her? Admire her? Is he scared of her? Is he going to lash out at her?

Unconcerned for her safety, Meredith continues to bore in, "The people together, collectively, have power and you know it. Why won't you admit that the bombs, tanks, those kinds of weapons don't represent power, not true power. No, they are weak and ineffectual symbols of power, just like money. History proves over and over that weapons cannot and never will break the spirit and will of the people." Spent, Meredith allows for several moments of silence. Then she claws back but with a calm assurance, "I never tire of analyzing why I do what I do and why I've done what I've done. I suspect you are the same. I have some peyote. Will you go on a vision quest with me?" Derrick flinches. Meredith sees him waver. "What, don't have the balls to look deep into who you are? What you are? Why you are? Thought you were a tough guy." Meredith swallows a handful of peyote buttons. She muses while she waits for the effect. A beautiful summer evening in this gorgeous Blue Grass country. They both remain still under the vast twinkling night sky. Minutes pass. Meredith's stomach kicks. She grimaces. Another kick. She gags. She takes deep breaths. She's overwhelmed by the surrounding beauty. The trees, the stars, the bright moon that seems to be within arm's length. She exhales a slow, deep lament, "When, when, oh, when will we all come together?" She talks at Derrick quietly, gently, "Imagine, imagining, imagination!!! That's real power. Nothing compares," she whispers. The fire reaches for the sky. Time vanishes. Two minutes later? An hour later? The past, the present and the future dogpile, piggyback, intertwine. Staring hard at Quince Meredith sucks in air and gulps, "Wetiko!" Derrick recoils but tries gamely to keep his poker face. Meredith closes her eyes and says matter of fact, "Hurt people, hurt people," she lets a few seconds pass, then points into the flames, "Your father apologizes to you."

Startled, Derrick exhales, "What?" He looks deeply into the fire. He can see him. His father. "I'm sorry, son. Truly sorry. Oh, how sorry. I hurt you."

"Daddy, Daddy...," sobs Derrick.

Meredith repeats several times, "He beat you. He beat you."

Tears stream down Derrick's face. He tucks his head between his knees, "Yes, yes. The horror."

"Forgive him and you will be free. You are a man among men. You must forgive," Meredith entreats.

Derrick stares blankly, "I need forgiveness. It's me. I've been passing on misery to others because of him. But I forgive. I do. I am so sorry," he utters plaintively.

Incredibly these two opposites in so many beliefs have shared a vision. Two leaders coming together.

Even more incredibly Derrick Quince has flipped. He shares Meredith's vision of a world coming together peacefully.

Jubilee 2020 will take place as scheduled.

Unless, of course, there is a deep state.

End of Chapter 12

Part 1. **#Jubilee Fever 2020**